To Richard Castellano

With
best wishes from

Claudia
Cragg

THE NEW TAIPANS

A VITAL SOURCE BOOK ON THE PEOPLE AND BUSINESS OF THE PACIFIC RIM

CLAUDIA CRAGG

CENTURY
BUSINESS
BOOKS

First published by Century Ltd
Random House, 20 Vauxhall Bridge Road, London SW1V 2SA

Random House Australia (Pty) Limited
20 Alfred Street, Milsons Point, Sydney
New South Wales 2061, Australia

Random House New Zealand Limited
18 Poland Road, Glenfield
Auckland 10, New Zealand

Random House South Africa (Pty) Limited
PO Box 337, Bergvlei, South Africa

Random House UK Limited Reg. No. 954009

Papers used by Random House UK Limited are natural, recyclable products made from
wood grown in sustainable forests. The manufacturing processes conform to the
environmental regulations of the country of origin.

ISBN 0 7126 61328

Printed and bound in Great Britain by
Mackays of Chatham PLC, Chatham, Kent

Contents

Acknowledgements

A great many people have been of invaluable help over the past 15 years in putting this book together. Of these, my greatest debt both personally and professionally is to Anthony L. T. Cragg. I am especially grateful also to Patrick Walsh, Simon King, and Elizabeth Hennessy. Of the dozens of people who gave invaluable professional insight and help, particular mention must be made of Claire Barnes, Angus Baxter, (Smith New Court), Graham Catterwell, (Crosby), G. K. Goh, Mark Greenwood, Keng Loke, (Kim Eng), Chek Lo, (Smith New Court), Duncan Mount, (CEF (HK)), Stewart and Grace Palmer, (Ord Minnett), Sashi Thapa, Tim Voake, (Peregrine), and Richard T. Weiss, (Strong Funds – USA). Thank you also to Mary Beth Shea, Linda Pulkowski, Lisa Claffey, Kate Stone and the staff at ULS Hartland.

Note: Figures expressed in dollars ($) refer to US dollars unless otherwise indicated.

Chapter 1

Celestial Empire versus Outer Barbarians

In James Clavell's bestselling novel *Tai-Pan*, set in Hong Kong in 1841, the 'supreme ruler' of the title was a nineteenth-century Englishman called Dirk Struan. *The New Taipans* documents the true story of the commercial experiences and histories of individuals in cities throughout South-East Asia over the last four decades. For the most part, the key players are overseas Chinese businessmen and women. As Singapore's Lee Kuan Yew has stated: 'We are ethnic Chinese but our stakes are in our own countries, not China where our ancestors came from.' This small group of powerful people, who are bound together by the most indefinable and elite of networks, now rule the greatest part of twentieth-century Asia. Indeed, all the indications are that they could very soon rule world trade.

At first glance, the business qualities of the new taipans are not dissimilar to those of any of the West's outstanding business heroes. Key amongst these attributes is a persistent attention to detail that can be seen in such figures as Lee Iacocca, Lord Hanson and Rupert Murdoch. Many of the new taipans have been exposed for years to the Western way of business, and thus are consummate practitioners in it. They are also usually active in most of the world's stock markets and the listed companies, not just in those of their immediate locale. Some have even been through such well-known US business schools as Harvard and Columbia. What sets this group apart, however, is an unusually keen sense of entrepreneurial adventure and an appetite for risk-taking that established commercial giants would dismiss as foolhardy. Not for the taipans the Western obsession with number-crunching and the bottom line. One other important trait of the taipan and his business operation is the significance throughout day-to-day operations of family involvement. Key accountancy and

1

management responsibilities are entrusted exclusively to blood relatives or the closest and oldest of friends.

The title of 'taipan' is accorded, by mutual unspoken agreement, only to those considered worthy of great respect, in the strictest of Confucian definitions. This respect is for business acumen and achievement. Although the hierarchy of the taipans has never been formally defined by wealth, power or territory, it is tacitly understood by both the business community and Oriental society at large. A powerful but tyrannical businessman who might get to the top in cultures such as the United States, Italy or Japan will necessarily fail to make the grade of taipan if he lacks a strict ethical base in Confucian morality. It is important to emphasise here the gulf between Confucian and Western morality. Some business dealings which are acceptable to the taipans would generally be considered by the West to be rather improper. This Oriental behaviour is not born out of some heightened sense of right and wrong: it is a convenient device to ensure that shame of any kind is never brought on the company which will cause it to lose standing or 'face'.

Similarly, the original taipans – who were British – did not necessarily subscribe to conventional standards of behaviour. As Jan Morris says in her outstanding book, *Hong Kong: Epilogue to an Empire*, 'they have often been interesting, often courageous and generally enterprising but not habitually overflowing with the milk of human kindness'.

When applied to corporate life in nineteenth-century Hong Kong, the term 'taipan' described exclusively the expatriate – frequently Scottish – heads of the giant foreign trading companies. These 'hongs', as the Chinese called such organisations, included Butterfield Swire, Jardine Matheson, and Russell & Company. Perhaps the most memorable of the original taipans was William Jardine, one of the Guangzhou merchant scions of the house of Jardine Matheson. He was known locally as 'the Iron-Headed Old Rat'.

Using the treaty ports on the China coast as a base for their business, these first taipans catered to the needs of both the expatriate and the Chinese populations, providing essential services such as banking, accountancy, shipping, insurance, and the supply of every conceivable durable and perishable commodity. The 'Big Boss' ('tai pan' in Chinese) was always obeyed without question and made sure that he knew everything and everyone, so that his control was supreme and inviolate. It was universally understood that if anyone stepped out of line, the taipan's commercial favours would be with-drawn, causing incalculable long-term harm. Vindictiveness and ret-ribution played no part in dealings, since too much time had to be spent in mere survival. The contemporary code of honour was based on practical commercial rather than social chivalry. In nineteenth- and early twentieth-century Asia, the taipans cheerfully acknowl-edged their social and political responsibilities, the greatest of which was a sense of duty to those with whom business was done.

Until comparatively recently no Chinese could be said to have reached the heights of taipan, even though his sphere of influence, and the contents of his wallet, may ostensibly have warranted it. This was not only for reasons of racism but also because the skills and capacities of the Chinese at that time were better suited to behind-the-scenes matters. The Chinese who sought influence in the community often acted as 'compradors' or interlocutors for the taipans rather than as sole traders or merchants working for them-selves. They had not yet reached the bi-cultural commercial literacy that now allows them control over both business domains.

At that time, the Chinese conducted themselves in what in retro-spect could be considered a somewhat demeaning but successfully opportunistic manner. After the political upheavals in China in 1949, these Chinese go-betweens were frequently criticised by the Communist Party as 'imperialist running dogs'. They nevertheless behaved with intelligence, composure and not a little business cun-ning. New skills were forced upon them out of necessity, an inevit-able consequence of the clash of the two alien cultures. Foremost of these was the new flexibility in business thinking and an appreci-ation of Western ways of commerce. If there was money to be made, reasoned the Chinese, their supreme ability as traders and deal-makers would surely come in useful.

This nineteenth-century business legacy has stood today's new taipans in good stead and helps to explain what is known as the 'banana' syndrome. Surprisingly never a pejorative term, and largely used by the Chinese themselves, the phrase describes those who are without question Asian on the outside but comparatively 'white' within, who have a foot, and when they want it a soul, in both cultures. A number of today's exceptional Chinese businessmen – such as David Li, of the Bank of East Asia, Dickson Poon of Dickson Concepts, or the larger-than-life David Tang – are for all the world typical British gentlemen.

David Tang is not only a habitual cigar-smoker of the most immodest Havana type, but he also owns the entire Asian franchise for them. It is perhaps only his exuberance that gives him away as a consummate Chinese deal-maker. Sitting in his Eaton Square flat or in one of the St James's clubs of which he is a member, he is surrounded by more British social trappings than the most quintessential of Englishmen. In his Savile Row pinstripes and with his clipped Oxford accent, he is more English than the English. His connections at the very highest level in mainland China, throughout South-East Asia and in England and America, however, soon dispel any illusion that he is anything other than the most faithful and best connected Chinese.

The rare ability of the Chinese to parody themselves does not in any way detract from the very serious and far-reaching nature of their business involvements. The observer is left wondering whether businesspeople of this genre are really Chinese or whether they are 'gweilo' (or 'foreign devil', as white men were called). They are, of course, both, ostensibly being intellectual and emotional hybrids, deferential to both camps and expert in all necessary skills.

Tang is not alone, nor is his kind confined to Hong Kong. The colonial connection has been only one of many catalysts in the evolution of business and the manner in which it is conducted. Nevertheless Hong Kong can boast three of the world's richest men, according to 1994's Forbes Top 25. Lee Shau Kee, at number thirteen in the list, was estimated to have net assets of $6.5 billion. In fourteenth place were the Kwok brothers, with $6.4 billion, while Li Ka-Shing, twenty-second in the list, was worth $5.8 billion.

Other cities in the region, such as Kuala Lumpur, Bangkok, Singapore, Jakarta, Manila and Taipei, all have their own tycoons, though some live a determinedly low-profile life. Taiwan appeared in the top ten, with the Tsai family – ranked ninth – commanding estimated net assets of $7.5 billion. Asia now has forty-six tycoons outside Japan, compared with only fourteen in 1987. Many have been so successful that they have been honoured with decorations of the highest order, such as the knighthoods given to cinema magnate Sir Run Run Shaw and to Sir Robert Ho Tung.

Emigrés and refugees around the world are used to such cultural schizophrenia, and the overseas Chinese are no exception. They frequently find their allegiance divided, some between mainland China (even though they might never have been there) and the land where they find themselves living, others between two opposing religions. In general they manage to encompass both loyalties, and in doing so, synthesise, for the most practical of reasons, a new way of doing business. And when the time is right, as it is now with the emergence of China as an economic supergiant, this approach reaps untold economic benefits and poses minimal risks.

When Clavell's novel was published in the late sixties, Western public opinion was only just beginning to wake up from its cultural chauvinism. Unfashionable though it was, the idea had begun to take root that there might be civilisations west of the Tuscan Hills worthy of further study. The first non–Occidental culture to impinge on our consciousness was Japan, which by the late 1970s was beginning to show its commercial mettle. It was to our advantage to study the Japanese so that business dealings with that country might become less awkward. Not until very recently, however, has it occurred to the West that other cultures in Asia also offer increasingly lucrative markets. There is life after Japan, now that she is beginning to suffer the maturity pains of even the greatest economies. Before too long, the collective investment flow of the overseas Chinese will be greater than that of the Japanese.

The inevitable movement of the epicentre of world business from one continent to another has attracted a great deal of attention to China. The school of demographic economic possibilities has maintained for some time that a market like China, with one billion-plus people and all the associated countries that surround it, must be worth pursuing. They argue that if every Chinese were to eat a McDonald's each day, or even just one a week, the revenue earned would annihilate all domestic economic problems with one fell swoop. Until very recently, China, in serious stagnation for at least thirty years, refused to enter the commercial arena. When, with the final death knell of the Cultural Revolution, the authorities opened the doors to a fledgling market economy by allowing workers to grow extra crops for sale for personal profit, the capitalist bug took hold.

In the late 1990s, it is a pandemic. For the first time for many young mainland Chinese realisation has dawned that, contrary to all the Maoist propaganda they had been fed, the best, and perhaps the only way to boost flagging production is through personal profit incentive and a market economy. Lining your own pockets is now not only officially sanctioned but heartily endorsed for the good of the country and the Party. Centralised planning and totalitarian social policies have gradually been discredited. The fruits of this new freedom, the once rare pair of Rayban sunglasses and the tailored leather jacket, are now worn with pride from Canton to Chungking. The enthusiasm for money-making has spread from its agrarian roots into every conceivable form of manufacturing and deal-making and has fanned out in concentric circles to envelop all the major cities of Asia and beyond.

The days when mighty Japan unquestionably dominated the lands of the Asian-Pacific may not be over yet, but few would disagree that the country's regional hegemony is not what it once was. The parlous state of the yen–US dollar exchange rate has caused giant fissures to appear in both the American and Japanese economies. The less powerful countries in the region, which make up the ASEAN bloc (Association of South-East Nations) and are composed of myriad small companies, have been able to pile swiftly into the fray where once they would have been too timid to do so.

Although these countries are no longer dependent on Japan, they owe her a lasting debt of gratitude, since their post-war growth has been largely on the back of her success. It was after all the momentum of Japan's shift to overseas production that provided a much-needed stimulus to future development. Today, investment in the Asian-Pacific region by the four 'tigers' – Hong Kong, South Korea, Singapore and Taiwan – has all but swamped that of Japan.

When it comes to overseas commercial manoeuvring, the indigenous Chinese, or 'huaqiao', scattered throughout the region have a great advantage over the Japanese. Their inbuilt network of extended family and friends allows for instant business and investor relations throughout Asia and mainland China. The 'guanxi' (connections) are not based, as they often are in Japan, on commercial decisions reached via market research and surrogate business relationships, but are developed from tried and trusted value judgements formed sometimes over generations. The Chinese living in Hong Kong invariably have relatives and long-standing friends on the mainland, as do those in Taiwan, Singapore, Malaysia and Thailand. There is a further network, between Chinese in, say, Hong Kong and those in Indonesia, between Singapore Chinese and their contacts in Thailand. No familial tie, however loose it may be in practice, is overlooked if it might produce a lucrative business relationship.

6

The Japanese, isolated for so long in their 'one island, one people' mentality, can never hope to compete with these connections. Furthermore, their largely disparaging and racist attitude to anyone who is not 'hyaku-percento' (a hundred per cent Japanese) taints some local negotiations, however much they may now apologise for past war crimes. The rift created between Japan and her neighbours by the Second World War is still largely unhealed, despite the desire by some to jump on the yen bandwagon. Even the natural relationships between the people of Japan and the Japanese in, say, Hawaii or Brazil have produced only minimal new strands of commercial success.

The entrepreneurship of the new taipans is as much an attitude as it is a conscious policy or set of guiding principles. Instead of doubting the success of a particular course of action, the new taipan will characteristically follow through every project to its logical extreme, testing waters, making connections and ironing out difficulties along the way, until a perhaps unexpected conclusion is reached. A deal that might start out with the export of chicken feed to China can, bizarrely in Western eyes, transform itself into the establishment of a motorcycle plant – something that happened recently for Thai conglomerate C. P. Pokhphand. To a taipan, not bothering with the exploration because the germ of the idea might not ultimately bear fruit seems nonsensical. Often, the more outrageous or difficult a notion, the more likely he is to go for it. Only ten years ago, Dickson Poon would have been laughed at for wanting to develop the best retail stores in Shanghai and for wanting to buy Harvey Nichols out from under the British. No one is laughing now. His supreme belief in himself as a consummate deal-maker and the certainty of his 'guanxi' are universally admired by other taipans. They understand that his behaviour is not just bravado and that it is perhaps this very abundance of confidence that allows him to succeed.

For the taipans business is all or nothing. Intellectually they have much in common with Edward de Bono's lateral-thinking approach to a project, which embraces all possibilities, far-fetched or otherwise. This allows for maximum creativity, and of course for maximum failure. For this reason there have been some spectacular errors in every taipan's career. Given, however, that taipans rarely 'bet the ranch', these idiosyncratic commercial forays hardly ever turn out to be completely disastrous.

In his property dealings Li Ka-Shing has gone out on a limb over and over again, and has shown that those experiments that were considered duds can pay off in the long run. His Rabbit UK telephone venture for Hutchison, however, was a write-off which caused a great deal of mirth in some business quarters. It was a mistake, though, that Li could afford to make, since the loss was negligible compared with the size of the group or even the telecommunications division on its own. Li's out-on-a-limb strategic purchase of Husky Oil in Canada was also scorned for a long time but now looks as though it may well come good in the long run. Few laugh however at his outstanding satellite television venture, although this might prove equally prone to failure. There is no shame in the attempt: only in the failure to try.

For a taipan, failure has a purpose, in that it allows the kernel of a project to be honed down to essentials. By the time the tasks are completed, the methodology has been thoroughly explored for every possibility. This particularly applies to the practical implementation of projects against a legal framework and in foreign territories, where perhaps the commercial background is unstable or downright hostile. Areas or types of business which would be considered unethical in Western terms are often given close consideration, and risks are taken which lawyers in the West would counsel strongly against. The gambling element is considered an intrinsic business skill, and the success of a venture is measured as much by the means as by the ends.

Decision-making among the taipans is never a lengthy democratic process as it so often is in the West, but is based rather on the whim of an autocrat whose nose for profit has not been dulled by error. Education in all spheres – for self-improvement in the understanding of both facts and philosophies, for the stimulation of creative ideas and new directions for business, and for the very greatest possibilities for communication – is diligently pursued. Many overseas Chinese students attend colleges in the United States or Australia, not so much to see the way of life as to absorb that country's thought processes in order to achieve an invaluable bi-culturalism. However, the Western preoccupation with pigeonholing is reviled. To the Chinese, each man is a universalist who will use his common sense and the talents of those around him to do any job not just to the best of his ability but to the heights of possibility.

For centuries, Western writers have struggled to define the Oriental concept of 'face'. It is perhaps most accurately explained as a heightened sense of the most practical decorum both in business and in social dealings. This translates into a mode of behaviour that lies at the core of all the taipans' dealings. It prescribes conduct that might seem alien, unnatural or absurdly circumspect to those who are not of an Oriental mindset. Many of these so-called 'inscrutable' tenets, however, are not exclusively Chinese, or Japanese, but can be commonly found in any civilisations where the desire to avoid giving offence dictates social mores. It is often the degree that marks the difference. This code of conduct is especially important to the Chinese, largely because of the value they attach to the idea of personal pride. This sets them apart from the Japanese, who regard responsibility and pride as a collective rather than an individual trait.

It is in the subtle playing of the game of face that confusion and difficulty arise for Westerners. Anyone ignorant of the countless subtleties involved will quickly be made to look foolish. Loss of face can be brought about without the victim even being aware of it. In Western civilisations, where idiosyncrasy is frequently a highly prized virtue, personal pride is less important, and for Catholics is actually a sin. In Asia, a simple meal with a group of business associates can be a maze of subtle considerations. The seating arrangements, who first picks up his chopsticks, who gets the tastiest food from the most highly prized dish, and who pays, or is allowed to pay, the bill at the end all denote an individual's rank. Among the new taipans the distinctions and subtleties are all the more precise and are often invisible to the unpractised eye.

Ironically, the staggering success of the taipans today owes a great deal to the imperialist aspirations of the white man. The 'gweilo' commercial supremos of two hundred years ago set out to turn the then desolate islands of Hong Kong and other unfamiliar Asian cities into impregnable fortresses of colonial power. The result, they hoped, would be that each man would be rewarded for his intrepid daring with a life as unequivocal ruler of his own domain.

Hong Kong is now a booming centre for regional trade and home to some of the wealthiest of the rich and famous. It also houses, as do the other capital cities of Asia, some very distinctive business tycoons. Today's taipans wield financial influence on a scale that could never before have been imagined, and yet manage to remain cloaked in an anonymity that is the envy of the business giants of the West. With the advantages of modern travel and telecommunications, the territory ruled by these invisible commercial wizards knows no bounds. In their eyes, today's world has no economic borders, real or imaginary.

It is increasingly true that the world's economic centre in the 1990s lies, not as for so long on either side of the Atlantic, but among the cities and states of the Asian-Pacific Rim. These countries – Hong Kong, Singapore, Taiwan, Thailand, Malaysia, South Korea, Indonesia and Vietnam, and even Myanmar, Brunei, Laos and Cambodia – account for an increasingly large share of international commerce. The Asian-Pacific Rim represents the crucible of the new economic forces. With the highest growth rates in the world, averaging at around 8% p.a. growth in GDP in the last couple of years alone, this region has notably boosted its share of the international economy.

By the year 2000, East Asian economies will have a gross national product as big as North America's and greater than Europe's. However, this power shift from the Atlantic to the Pacific does not necessarily mean that America will automatically be consigned to second-class status in the economic sphere. On the contrary, such an enormous change presents vital opportunities. In the coming competition, the edge will belong to those nations and companies strong enough to nurture individual initiative, creativity, and quick decision-making. This lesson may be well learned from any businessman whose forefathers hailed from mainland China.

The evidence of this economic power shift is everywhere. In 1960, America's trade with Asia was just over half of that with Western Europe. During the next twenty years, trade with Asia outstripped that with Europe. By 1986, US trans-Pacific commerce reached $215 billion, exceeding by more than 50% its trade with Western Europe, and is still growing by leaps and bounds. If American trade with Asia continues to increase at current rates, as it undoubtedly will (a theory confirmed by, amongst others, a report by the Commission on Industrial Competitiveness), it will soon be twice that across the Atlantic. But changes are happening within America too.

Today the Pacific Basin countries constitute the largest source of new legal immigrants to the United States, with Europeans accounting for barely one in ten newcomers. The new non-European America constitutes a growing percentage of the nation's skilled workforce. By the mid-1980s, non-whites accounted for more than 40% of all freshmen at the University of California at Berkeley, with a majority of them Asian and a large percentage of them Chinese. Across the continent, 14% of all new entrants at Harvard University in 1987 were Asian-Americans. What is more, Asians account for nearly 70% of all foreign engineering doctorate recipients, many of whom choose to stay after graduation, thus enriching America's technology companies. Taiwan, for instance, has sent nearly 100,000 students to the United States for graduate degrees. Of the 10,000 who earned PhDs, 85%, including several eventual Nobel Prize winners, have remained in America.

The first step for the West in building a successful business future must be to redefine our relationship with the world's eastern hemisphere and with countries other than Japan. The basis for this new relationship will be the forty million overseas Chinese who live strewn throughout the Asian-Pacific Rim and who have, between them, a GNP two-thirds the size of that of the 1.1 billion people in Communist China. The economic culture of a dramatic cast of just 150 interlinked Chinese entrepreneurs, the new taipans, and their family businesses has generated this vast wealth.

The new taipans, almost exclusively overseas Chinese, are revered and feared throughout the commercial world. About fifteen key individuals will soon constitute the most potent economic power outside Japan. Some believe the influence of this group, with the eventual revitalisation of mainland China, will outwit and outperform even Japan's economic might. Lee Kuan Yew, the former Prime Minister of Singapore and himself Chinese, expressed the opinion that 'the Pacific Basin is the region with the greatest potential for development and growth for the next 100 years. What Japan has done, the other peoples along the Rim, Koreans, Chinese, Vietnamese, can do, though it may perhaps be less spectacular in results. The peoples of East Asia, about 1.25 billion people in all, have similar cultures with similar levels of pre-industrial civilisation as Japan.'

Although the networks of personal relationships through which the taipans operate are not always exclusively Chinese, the very successful ones are more likely to be predominantly Chinese or to work at some point significantly through a thoroughly Chinese commercial domain. The Japanese and the Koreans, however, also operate through similar systems and also have their taipans. Western businessmen should endeavour to become familiar with all of them. The different business pyramids – Korean, Japanese and Chinese –

11

distinguish three different business ethics but have a great deal in common and are largely interdependent.

Increasingly, the influence of these Chinese and other Asian business dynamos is moving far beyond the traditional Oriental spheres into domains that are largely considered the preserve of Western business. The family- and friends-based networks revolve around an ostensibly informal yet very efficient information system largely centred on Hong Kong. That city, with its freewheeling, laissez-faire attitude to business operations, based on British law, has for many years been the natural congregation point for commercial networks. If, come 1997, it should cease to exist as we now know it, then the taipans will simply shift their focus to another Asian city, perhaps Singapore, Bangkok or even Ho Chi Minh.

It has now become increasingly important for anyone in business to understand the mindset of these commercial dynamos. Readers of the endless stream of Japanese management titles may have a head start, but the Chinese have distinct rules of their own. The business fundamentals of the new taipans are based on the principles of the importance of the family structure, the work ethic and filial piety. For centuries, Chinese entrepreneurs have successfully negotiated the tightrope of government authority and somehow thrived. Now, as overseas Chinese, freed of the millstone of tradition, their business empires boom, as is borne out by the success stories emanating from the varied cultural and economic structures of Taiwan, Malaysia, Singapore, and Indonesia. The taipans' empires, interlinked by the common bonds of family and friendship, grow outward and upward, gradually and imperceptibly encompassing the globe.

Chapter 2

Japan as Number Two

Recession, deflation and the subsequent effect on land prices have hit Japan hard. The shock was compounded because some were beginning to be convinced of the nation's invincibility. Most economists now predict that Japan's annual GDP growth won't exceed 3% in the foreseeable future. Traditional markets, at home and abroad, are becoming more competitive than ever. Other problems facing Japan in the mid-1990s include the continuing woes of the ruling Liberal Democratic Party and a creeping awareness that Japan Inc. is somehow, and perhaps surprisingly, managing to lose the quality battle to both the US and Germany.

In the past, Japan has had every reason to take pride in its manufacturing expertise and quality; now it is forced to re-evaluate every part of the process, from basic production techniques to management. Consequently, redundancies are widespread: Nissan's Zama plant laid off 4,000 workers while telecommunications giant NTT announced that it will let go 30,000 employees over three years. Reports of 'kata tataki', 'the tap on the shoulder' that precedes the Japanese pink slip, are growing. The lay-offs are usually Japanese-style: huge numbers of people with very little to do face a severe loss of overtime income and find themselves in danger of unemployment.

This situation is unprecedented for the Japanese economy. In the past, big companies would be restructured discreetly by their bankers, not allowed to go bust. The time-honoured system of lifetime employment is being eroded in favour of increased worker mobility, a result of three years of recession exacerbated by a very strong yen. The country has started to go through a programme of 'business re-engineering' designed to redistribute the domestic workforce into job-sharing and from a manufacturing culture to one that is more

13

service-based. One after another, major industries – mining, textiles, steel, shipbuilding – have moved out of Japan into cheaper territories. Textiles, for example, used to make up 30% of Japan's total exports, compared with just 2% today. Many products that the world thinks of as being 'Made in Japan' probably are not. Matsushita, for example, produces nearly all of its air-conditioners from a factory in Indonesia. As many as two out of every three Japanese televisions are today manufactured abroad.

Whether Japan likes it or not, there is no escape from the increasing likelihood, discussed in Chapter 1, that China will soon dominate as the biggest economic player in Asia and that Hong Kong, South Korea, Taiwan and Singapore will work hand in hand with Indonesia, Malaysia and Thailand to secure Chinese hegemony in the region. The commercial stars of Japan, who come largely from the 'zaibatsu' system, are all too well aware of the importance of the overseas Chinese taipans and of how in many ways they are beginning to beat the Japanese at their own game. To counter this trend, Japan has adopted a positive policy to try and integrate some of the best of South-East Asia into its economic empire. Several industries are targeted, the most notable of which is car manufacturing.

With a nominal GDP of around $3 trillion, Japan's economy is by far the largest in Asia. It now lies embedded in an East Asian economic community with an additional productive capacity of more than $1 trillion, and growing. Despite sincere economic overtures and investment in mainland China, Japan has found itself overtaken by overseas Chinese investment, and in some cases investment from the US. It is now a very real possibility that an emerging 'Greater China' and not Japan will come to dominate the Asian-Pacific region of the future.

Not so long ago, Japan's leaders put forward the idea of a Japan-centric 'Asian System', a powerful region in which Hong Kong, Singapore, Taiwan, South Korea, and perhaps even China, Malaysia, Thailand and Indonesia, would all defer, at least economically, to Tokyo. Such a scenario is now unlikely ever to take place. It is true that for the last fifteen years there has been a stream of 'the Japanese are coming' books published in the West, coupled with a publicity campaign depicting Japan as a menace hellbent on global domination, but the reality is very different.

While the West may be rather slow when it comes to direct investment in Asia, Japanese companies have been making a concerted effort to establish themselves throughout the region. A government directive was issued which encouraged companies to explore all potential for Asian expansion. The high growth rate of countries in the region, together with relatively low wages and a skilled workforce, makes for an economic opportunity that is too good to ignore. This push by Japan comes at a time when both American and European companies seem to be cutting back on Asian investment in favour of the newer emerging markets of South America and the old Eastern Europe and former Soviet Union.

Up until the middle of the nineteenth century, Japan borrowed heavily from the cultures of China and Korea. While persistently independent in politics, and quite isolated in its economy, the country is and always was indisputably Asian. Despite the ostensibly Western trappings that are in evidence the true American spirit has bypassed Japan. Even the degree of biculturalism that the taipans and other Chinese have achieved has eluded her. When Commodore Perry's 'black ships' arrived from America in 1853, Japan was made aware for the first time of the technological superiority of the West, which from then on would make both isolation and resistance more and more impossible. Japan reluctantly accepted that she must throw open her doors and accept Westernisation or be locked for ever in a semi-feudal existence.

By the time of the Meiji era, towards the end of the century, the country had both a stable, centralised political structure and a capitalist economy. The education system was efficient and productive and the armed forces were well equipped and highly trained. Regardless of her efforts, however, Japan knew that she was an outsider as far as the major civilisations of Europe and North America were concerned, considered by many to be racially inferior. It was then that a clamour arose from within the country calling for all things Western to be thrown out and for Japan to head the 'Asian family', though Japan's imperialistic view offered very little to Asian nations except subjugation of one sort or another. This clamour only ceased with defeat in 1945. Thereafter, especially in the mid sixties and early seventies, the mood swung back towards cultural and commercial symbiosis with the West. Similar mood swings, though for varying reasons, have occurred sporadically ever since.

It was not until the 1960s, when Second World War reparations had been settled, that Japan began to readdress her Asian concerns. At that time a number of countries in the region had thrown off their colonial yokes and gained independence. With foreign investment filtering through into the area, Japan started to reconsider its trade with Asia in the light of increasing friction in its more traditional markets. In the mid to late 1980s, when the yen was revalued and domestic inflation became an issue, renewed emphasis was placed on Asian trade. At the start of the 1990s trade with Asia constituted a full one-third of Japan's global dealings, more even than its trade with the US. At the same time the developing countries of Asia, in their eagerness to earn yen, focused on Japan as their main export market.

Many Japanese politicians subscribe to the 'flying geese' concept of Asian commerce created by economist Kaname Akamatsu. This envisages the Asian nations 'flying' in a V formation, with Japan at their head. It is intended to harness Japan's strengths with Asia's resources for the betterment of the whole. The quid pro quo, though, is that Japan, as spokesman and puller-of-strings, must remain the number one nation. The idea is that the Japanese should no longer think of themselves either exclusively as Asians or as members of the West, but should accept the hybrid nature that comes about from the two halves of their cultural and sociological personality. They need, it is argued, to find a new role in the Asian-Pacific region that will bring together East and West. This need is not being met.

The reality is that Japanese firms and the population at large are struggling to come to grips with the fallout from the bubble economy. Numerous Japanese companies have lost billions of yen in bad deals or in transactions eroded by the revaluing of their currency. For well over a decade, production facilities were continually expanded, and trillions of yen were spent on R & D, only to find that orders subsequently diminished and new projects, such as high-definition TV and fifth-generation intelligence, failed to fulfil their commercial promise. Meanwhile, financial institutions lent more and more money to encourage the commercial boom, only to find that today, in the mid 1990s, they face at least a $150 billion crisis of bad debt. Recent governments have refused to artificially boost the stock market, thus forcing companies to face up to the consequences of too much growth. As share prices have fallen, more and more companies have had to cut down production and waste, and turn to Asia, both as a source of labour and as a market.

The closest the world has yet seen to an Asian system of any kind is the attempt at a post–Cold War order through APEC, the proposed East Asian economic caucus. From Japan's point of view, the cooperation between herself and the ASEAN countries, with the future of the Asian-Pacific region in mind, is based on the building of a community of nations. This would embrace not only Japan and the states of South-East Asia, but all the nations that border on the Pacific – from north to south Pacific, and westward to the Americas as well. Japan takes great pride in its contribution to the growth of the ASEAN economies, and continually pledges increasing support for them. Her politicians express remorse over her wartime behaviour and pledge that the country will never again become a military power. In general, the Japanese have completely revised their previously vocal opinions of their own superiority and their sense of Asian exclusiveness. They are calling for cooperation within a global context, embracing the whole of the Asian-Pacific region but with the United States as the linchpin.

The importance of Japan's overseas aid programme to the region should not be underestimated. And this is before the wealth of investment from Japanese corporations and entrepreneurs is taken into account. At the end of the 1980s, Japan was donating nearly two-thirds of all available aid. To begin with, the focus for Japanese money was Hong Kong, Korea, Singapore and Taiwan. Then, as those countries developed, it moved on to mainland China, Indonesia, the Philippines, Malaysia and Thailand. By the end of the 1980s the programme was financially the healthiest of any country in the world, hovering around the $10 billion per annum mark.

Japan is also keen to see cooperative efforts to support economic development, an open trading system, arms restraint and democratisation. To help achieve all of this, they are seeking to strengthen other Pacific-wide regional institutions, such as the ASEAN Post Ministerial Conference (PMC) for the discussion of political and security issues.

At the same time Japan takes great pains to stress adherence to the mutual security treaty with the US. Japanese politicians repeatedly affirm that the presence of US security forces in Asia is indispensable. Recent prime ministers have emphasised the importance of maintaining a foot in both Asia and the West. While it is indisputably true, they have argued, that Asia is increasing in stature, the West, and particularly the United States, continues to be Japan's principal economic partner. Japan's trade with the West is considerably greater than her intra-Asian dealings, and the US is also the richest source of foreign investment. America also helps fund Japan's defence and justifies to the world at large the growth of Japan's military, 'for self-defence purposes to her neighbours'. What Japan wants more than anything is approbation from both the US and the European Union, so that she can achieve the global recognition she now feels is her due.

Over the last fifteen years, Japan has been attempting to absorb the Asian economies into its own network by providing what it sees as unparalleled managerial and commercial leadership, coupled with major industrial and corporate investment, frequently with long periods of interest-free loans. The formal scheme through which this policy is intended to be carried out was announced by the Ministry for International Trade and Industry (MITI) in 1987 under the title of 'the New Asian Industrial Development Plan'. As a result, major Japanese corporations ploughed their expertise and investment for the manufacture of luxury cars and microelectronics into countries which had previously produced mostly raw commodities. The focus up to now, as with the overseas aid programme, has been Hong Kong, Singapore, South Korea and Taiwan, and these four alone now produce over 10% of the world's manufactured goods. The United States produces 12%. More recently, corporate Japan has moved into Malaysia, Indonesia, the Philippines, Thailand, China and Vietnam, with the next projected stage involving India, Sri Lanka and Bangladesh. One of Japan's stated reasons for carrying out this plan has been that labour costs at home and the yen abroad have risen so fast that shifting to overseas production provides the only solution.

The position of each individual Asian-Pacific country *vis-à-vis* Japan is very much dictated by the attitude of that country's taipans. In Thailand, where new Japanese factories were said to be opening at a rate of one every three or four days, Japan is the number one overseas direct investor at around $2 to $4 billion per annum. In Malaysia, the Japanese have more than 250 different manufacturing ventures and since the liberalisation of investment laws have been allowed to own a number of operations outright. For the moment, it suits the new taipans to share in the industrial momentum. Japan's long-standing colonial and commercial ties with Taiwan and South Korea have stood her in good stead. Both countries import over half their high-technology components and goods from their old master.

In many cases, Japanese finance and expertise have helped decide upon which industrial sectors a country should concentrate, have drawn up the infrastructural plans and have then provided the capital to create the reality. The emphasis on training within each country came from an MITI department, the Association for Overseas Technical Scholarships, which allocated resources for technical cooperation and personnel. The blueprint envisaged a so-called 'Asian Brain', which would see the workforces of Asia harnessed by Japanese management, with MITI providing the coordination. What was not bargained for was the unexpected resistance from the new taipans, who were happy to ride the wave until the moment arrived for them to spin off their own entrepreneurial and highly individualistic empires.

Chapter 3

Paddy Fields Make Way for Parking Lots

The growth of capitalism in the Asian-Pacific Rim in the last two decades has all but left Western countries breathless. In the old days, pith-helmeted expatriates in Asia, relaxing with their Singapore Slings, took great comfort in the fact that as far as they were concerned East and West would never meet. The philosophies and values of the two worlds were just too different, they believed. Asia was merely a charming backwater that also happened to supply a great many valuable commodities.

Now, however, the East is setting the pace in terms of economic growth. According to the IMF, in the year 2000 half of the estimated gross world product of $7.5 trillion (in 1990 dollars) will be contributed by Asia. Cynics argue that this is just a one-off growth cycle: success, they say, will only be temporary. However, Asian growth rates, which nearly always approach the double-digit level, are showing no sign of slowing down.

Those once complacent expatriates, together with academics from all over the globe, must today be wondering where on earth this economic miracle came from. The situation has changed so dramatically that in an ironic reversal of the usual job migration, large numbers of Westerners are descending on Hong Kong in search of employment. As the colonial sun sets, it is white men who are providing the 'coolie' workforce in Hong Kong, often answerable to indigenous supervisors. Unskilled expatriates now face unprecedented competition in the job market from often better-educated and better-qualified bilingual locals.

In 1993 Hong Kong's per capita GDP, of £11,970, overtook that of the UK, at £9,016, and that gap is likely to grow. During the twenty-five-year period from 1960 to 1985, the real GDPs of Hong

Kong, Singapore, South Korea and Taiwan doubled every eight years. Malaysia, Thailand, Indonesia and China show similarly impressive progress, although their growth didn't begin until the late 1970s. There is no ignoring these figures, nor comparison with the West, since hundreds of thousands of visiting businessmen have now seen for themselves the frenetic commercial activity in these Asian countries.

Even the economically uninformed observer notices everywhere examples of the dramatic rise in the standard of living and technological advancement in the East. Asia has been transformed into a series of modern megalopolises with skyscrapers to rival the very best of those in Houston: indeed, many of them have been designed by top American architects. People live in far better, often less expensive houses than the average European and seem to want for very little in the way of quality consumer durables and leisure services.

Remarkably, this metamorphosis has occurred at a time of comparative social and political instability. In 1987, for example, South Korea was beset by general strikes and the continuing threat from her northern neighbour, yet still managed to boost exports so that her trade surplus grew from $3.1 billion in 1986 to $6.9 billion. Japan, the big but not always so benevolent brother of the Asian nations, has also been experiencing its worst problems for the last thirty years, in the form of political schism and the rising yen. Despite this, the Japanese trade surplus with the United States shows few signs of shrinking.

If the taipans, as individuals and corporate heads, and their countries collectively can pull themselves up so magnificently by the bootstraps, there must be lessons here for the rest of us to learn. How has Asia done it?

Although it would be wrong to put the achievements down purely to policy, government or corporate, it is true that in each case there have been federal programmes instituted for widespread industrial planning, as well as some very favourable lures to attract foreign investment. Education has a high priority in all the governments' plans, with a heavy emphasis on giving young people the technological know-how they will need to cope with constantly changing times. In the Asian media there is a great deal of criticism of Western standards of general education, especially with regard to literacy.

Children in Asia are brought up to fear and respect their teachers, an attitude which is then transferred on to their employers. There is no question of doing anything other than your very best, because to fail would be to bring shame upon oneself and one's family. Asian mothers take their duties as 'support teachers' very seriously, providing the sort of encouragement and help that Western children seldom have access to. Since quasi-arranged marriages are common throughout many Asian countries, so-called 'dysfunctional' families are rare, and a stable home life is the norm. The main enemy is poverty, and with little in the way of welfare available, fear of penury keeps people working as hard as they possibly can.

There is no doubt that Asia's real advantage is this cultural one. The key factor is not ministries, planning or even funding, but attitude. The secondary factor is a large enough population willing to work with the growth. These factors apply equally to the transformation of corporations in the East.

A further issue to be considered in any discussion about Asian economic success is that of personal freedom. The new taipans are all determined autocrats who brook very little corporate democratic nonsense. They happen to find themselves, luckily for them, in societies that all too willingly complement their dispositions. However, time and again in Asia we have seen economic growth lead to political relaxation. This has been especially true in Taiwan and Korea, where so far, blooming democracy has not yet thwarted economic progress. It has not been the case, though, in mainland China, where runaway economic growth, post-Tiananmen, has not contributed to greater freedom as yet.

Even in the more liberal countries, however, levels of freedom, whether for an individual in society or an employee in a corporation, are very limited compared with the United States or the countries of Western Europe. In America, the most sacred democratic tenet is the right of the individual. People in the countries of the Asian-Pacific Rim take it for granted that they have restricted freedom and little autonomy, and are just cogs in the national or commercial wheel. To us it is an unpalatable fact that for these apparently subjugated peoples, less choice for the individual has, up till now, meant greater success for the country as a whole.

There is, furthermore, very little impetus for mass social change or politicisation. From the moment an Asian enters kindergarten as a child, till the day he dies, after perhaps many years in business, all personal choices are made according to the wishes of his 'superiors'.

Anyone who is older, who has been with the company longer, who has a more demanding job, is considered superior. There is no escape: someone, somewhere is always in a preferred position to your own. As hard as we may find it to believe, individuality of any kind is neither sought nor encouraged. In the interests of conformity, 'the nail that stands up must be banged down', for the economic benefit of all.

The taipans alone set themselves apart, by both behaviour and commercial achievement. Among a vast population, theirs is a very privileged position, one that depends on large numbers of cogs doing exactly what they are told, precisely when they are told to do it. It has been said that if the whole population of China – more than one billion people – were ordered to jump up and down, they would not only do so but would jump at exactly the same time. The likely Western response, in contrast, would be to first evaluate the worthiness of the request and then substantiate its rationale.

No amount of repression in a society is desirable, but without it, would Asia today be as economically successful as it is? Efficiency can only be achieved through smooth systems and operations, with no room for frequent changes of direction to accommodate individual whims. Complete or totalitarian control, though, is not the answer either. It is the happy medium in Asia that has allowed such an impressive level of continued growth.

Job mobility is generally discouraged in the East, but in countries like Taiwan, where there is a severe labour shortage, there is very little employers can do to stop valuable skilled workers being poached. There are, however, various subtle ways of keeping a grip on people. In Korea, for example, overseas travel has been made very difficult, except for those taking business trips. Until recently, anyone wishing to travel for pleasure has found it hard even to get a passport. In Singapore, tight controls are maintained on personal spending but there is a stipulation that all nationals must put a significant percentage of their income into the national retirement fund. In both cases, the greater good is put before the wishes of the individual, and with very little complaint.

This philosophy is also applied to the employment of women. It is taken for granted in Asian households that the man, unless incapacitated in some way, will be the lifelong breadwinner. The woman is merely a subsidiary wage-earner. This is not so much chauvinism, although it can be interpreted that way, as downright necessity. All but the top 2 or 3% of women are invisibly barred from the highest echelons of business, education and politics – most notably by their own self-imposed glass ceiling.

In all the societies where the new taipans flourish, property is predominantly in the hands of corporations and private individuals rather than the state. Similarly, the most important investment policies and decisions are handled by a handful of key corporate executives. The result is a society pulled ever upwards by the powerful traction of a number of constituent successes. Corporations do not consciously shore each other up against the bad times. There is no particular agenda or national commercial concert in the timing or making of decisions, or in gauging their effects on society. This is pretty much how business is done in the West, except that in Asia there is one major intrinsic assumption: personal freedom, while important, is instantly dispensable if in the long run it is considered that everyone will do better without it.

According to economists such as Yu-Shan Wu of the Brookings Institution, Japan differs significantly from the rest of Asia in this respect. It has a strong background administration in the guiding and string-pulling of bodies like MITI and the Keidanren, even though companies are predominantly in private or stockholders' hands. Bureaucracy regulates the degree of corporate idiosyncracy. Wu believes that this 'public-private' approach will have long-term advantages over the 'private-private' systems of the West. The taipans' corporations, for the most part, fly solo.

One of the distinct advantages of the public-private system is that a country can ensure it has at least a presence in all key sectors. The taipans operate their corporate economies in a similar way, though without the bureaucratic intervention. They will embark on ventures not necessarily because a pay-off is guaranteed, but because the expertise acquired will pay subsequent dividends in unexpected ways. This style combines the very best of Asian quick wit and decision-making with the more familiar advantages of the Western multinational. The approach is a hybrid containing elements from both East and West, and contributes to the process of continuing growth in Asia.

Since labour in their own countries is no longer cheap, the taipans are today looking to expand their operations outside Asia, and this global style enables them to do so. They are transferring to their new territories the technology they have come to acquire, along

24

with their Asian corporate wisdom, and are becoming lords of a far greater realm.

The growth of massive export-led business triggered a revolution in most of the taipans' own operations, a revolution which has changed them over twenty years from self-contained single-commodity or single-service companies into almost unchallengeable billion-dollar-plus world-class conglomerates. Some of the companies are now in fact groups of several businesses, owned and run by a consortium of families. Some are government-controlled. Whatever their make-up, all the corporations have taken their Japanese and Western competitors by surprise.

The Asian magnates' business methods are discussed more fully in Chapter 4, together with an evaluation of their corporate style. At first glance, however, we can see how their companies benefited from cheap labour and the changing nature of the economy of the country in which they found themselves. These companies, each headed by a taipan, exemplify a distinctive style of business that has developed since the 1970s.

There are some remarkable examples throughout the region of what are now highly diversified companies under the direction of a new taipan. They all started with a single, solid strand of business, yet today are major players on the world commercial stage. Despite the years of compound growth, some of the companies remain firmly under the control of the founding family.

The 'taipan's taipan', sixty-three-year-old Li Ka-Shing, reigns supreme over his group, the Hong Kong property-based empire, Cheung Kong. The company is principally involved in investment holding and project management, with subsidiaries in estate agency, cement and quarry operation and the production of ready-mixed concrete. With profits of over $1 billion per annum, it outperforms such world-renowned giants as Toshiba and Nissan. Li Ka-Shing personally has a 40% share of the ownership, and yet the majority of Westerners have never even heard of him. More interesting, perhaps, is the fact that the wealthiest man in Hong Kong pays himself an annual director's fee of only $641.

Through Cheung Kong, Li controls the giant conglomerate Hutchison Whampoa, which is heavily involved in telecommunications, the utility company Hongkong Electric, and a holding company, Cavendish. Hutchison's annual return on equity has averaged 19% per annum over the past decade. Although he is said to have a personal fortune in the region of $4 billion, Li has lived in the same house for over thirty years and has very modest tastes. He used to collect jade as a hobby, until he lost a piece and promptly gave up.

Although, strictly speaking, Michael Kadoorie should be classed as an old taipan proper – he is a 'gweilo' and the son of the late Lord Kadoorie – he has all the hallmarks of a new taipan. With a controlling interest in the Hong Kong & Shanghai Hotels group, who own the Peninsula chain, 34% of China Light & Power and 21% of Hong Kong Carpet, forty-one-year-old Kadoorie is worth approximately $3 billion. His grandfather, Sir Elly, left Baghdad in 1880 and moved to Shanghai to take up a clerical position in a relative's company. Apocryphal or not, the story goes that Elly was so disgusted with the state of the office that he dared to wash it down with disinfectant, and was promptly fired. That was all the incentive he needed to start his own business on the back of an uncle's $80 loan. Michael Kadoorie's inheritance is witness to his success.

A superb example of Asian corporate growth is that of the C. P. Pokhphand group in Thailand, a vast and secretive agro-industrial conglomerate with operations in more than a hundred companies around the globe. The business was set up in 1921, in a small back-street shop, by the father of the present CEO Dhanin Chearavanont, who is an overseas Chinese. It began by selling chicken feed and is now involved in everything to do with birds, including processing, breeding, feeding and distributing.

Having dominated the sector in Thailand, C. P. has now moved on through the peninsula and out into fields as far away as mainland China and Turkey, branching out into commodity trading and such commercially unrelated projects as the building in Belgium of a $400 million petrochemical plant for the manufacture of plastic containers. Continuing with the food theme, the company has linked up with Kentucky Fried Chicken for franchises not only on C. P.'s home turf in Bangkok, but also in China, and has recently got into sausages with Oscar Meyer and prawns with Japan's Mitsubishi. C. P. is also involved in brewing with Heineken and in motorbike production in mainland China. Furthermore, together with British Telecom, the company has established a venture that will treble the number of telephone lines in Thailand. As keen entrepreneurs there is nothing that they will not turn their hands to if the opportunity is right.

Thailand has a number of other conglomerates, all family-con-trolled, that are potentially of international note. They have recently been growing by leaps and bounds during a period of unprecedented economic success for Thailand. At one stage in the last five years it was the fastest-growing economy in the world.

The Bank of Ayudhya, Thailand's fifth-largest bank, and Siam City Cement, the country's second-largest cement producer, are both controlled by seventy-four-year-old Chuan Ratanarak. An immigrant from southern China at the age of six, Ratanarak began his working life as a docker and went on to establish his own business loading ships.

The Saha Pathana group, a similarly structured family-owned company, run by eight of Thiam Chokwatana's sons, is engaged in the trading and manufacturing of everything from detergent to lingerie, through more than five dozen companies. The last reported net profit margin was 30%. For the moment, the designated new taipan for the group is the third son, Boonsithi, who is taking on the challenge successfully enough to lick such competition as Colgate, Procter & Gamble and Unilever in some areas of business. With the cooperation of Japanese partners, the group is branching out successfully into other sectors.

Another instance of a conglomerate that has sprung out of banking origins is that of Bangkok Bank, which has recently seen a family of seven heirs squabble amongst themselves to decide who should control the company. The founder, Chin Sophonpanich, died six years ago, and has been succeeded, it would appear, by Chatri Sophonpanich, his second son. The family-controlled collection of companies has interests in a number of diverse areas, including hospitals and palm oil plantations. Chin must have known what might happen after his death, because he took great pains to structure the corporate organisation so that no one heir could hold majority control in any company and thus possibly destroy it. Perhaps he was aware of the fate of the once-powerful Tejapaibul family. With valuable assets in distilleries, brewing and banking, as well as property, the Tejapaibuls were once a force to be reckoned with. No longer. The ten sons virtually destroyed the business with their greedy squabbling.

Thaksin Shinawatra, Thailand's top telecommunications tsar and head of an empire now threatening to assume world proportions, is non-Chinese, a rarity both in the ranks of the taipans and among top Thai businessmen. Also unusually, Shinawatra is a former police-man, who hails originally from Chiang Mai and who began in business with the distribution of IBM computers. He set up Thailand's first cable television operation, and has also established his own cellular telephone network.

Siam Cement is in a league of its own in Thailand. Anything to do with the king in that country is considered sacred, and Siam Cement is 40% owned by the King's Crown Property Bureau. The company was started in 1913 by King Rama VI and today embraces around fifty diverse companies. Paron Israsena is taipan of the company, and is a true autocrat who sees no need to share with his stockholders information about the business. It is said too that the company underreports its earnings. Under Paron's very capable direction, however, business has continued to expand to the manufacture of car engines and construction materials, and to ventures in the petrochemical sector. There are also joint projects with a Michigan-based company, Guardian Industries, for the manufacture of plate glass, with Japan's Asahi Glass and Mitsubishi Electric, and with Dow Chemical.

Sime Darby, the formerly British cocoa, palm oil and rubber company, is now a taipan-run but state-controlled transnational enterprise, with regional ventures in everything from property development and lucrative BMW dealerships to the production of bathtubs. One of the company's most interesting international ventures is through a British condom manufacturer, Dur-A-Vend, the maker of the 'Do it in a Jiffy' prophylactic.

The unlikely taipan in question is a sixty-two-year-old Malay prince, 'Tunku' Ahmad Yahaya, an accountant by training and a graduate in economics from Bristol University. Based in Kuala Lumpur, his company is one of the region's pre-eminent manufacturing and trading conglomerates, with an annual equity return of around 19.6%. While the company escaped formal nationalisation in 1975, a large chunk of controlling shares was nevertheless acquired by the Malaysian government through the London Stock Exchange. Today, the government holds a full one-third of the shares, while some 6% of the company is owned by Kuwaiti interests. Day-to-day operations, however, are generally not interfered with.

The autocratic chairman of Taiwan's Formosa Plastics group is seventy-four-year-old Wang Yung-ching. His part-public, part-private conglomerate employs over 45,000 workers and is the world's number one producer of PVC (polyvinyl chloride). More often than not he can be found having lunch with his co-workers, even though, with more than a dozen manufacturing sites in the US alone, he is probably Taiwan's pre-eminent new taipan, rewarded with pre-tax annual profit margins around the 30% level.

Wang had little formal education, starting out in the rice and timber business when he was just fifteen. His son, however, who will undoubtedly succeed him as taipan, is British-educated, with a PhD in chemistry from London's Imperial College.

While Japan's 'sogo-shosha' – the trading and manufacturing companies which together make up the 'zaibatsu' system of financial giants and conglomerates – are a well-known phenomenon, South Korea's equivalent, the 'chaebols', are less widely appreciated. They are involved in the general manufacture of paper and pharmaceuticals, food production and, of course, electronics. Some of the best known are Lucky-Goldstar, Samsung, Hyundai and Daewoo, and several are taipan-run. With the days of Korea's head-to-head price war with Japan over, Korean conglomerates have followed the Japanese lead and moved a great part of the mainstream production overseas, throughout South-East Asia and as far as Mexico, in order to take advantage of lower wages.

A lesser-known 'chaebol' – but the one perhaps making the greatest international strides – is the Ssangyong group, which started out in cement. The core company itself has no production facilities but earned its revenue through trading oil, briquettes, steel and metal products. There are now five separate associated companies, dealing in cement, heavy industry (producing diesel engines and commercial vehicles) and paper (as the largest manufacturer of sanitary paper). Ssangyong became involved in the refining of oil in Korea and in a joint venture with the National Iranian Oil Company, which they subsequently bought out after the demise of the Ayatollah Khomeini. Surprising though it may seem, they were also behind the $400 million revitalisation of Singapore's Raffles City.

The taipan in this case is Kim Suk-Won, who at only forty-six is the youngest of his Korean peers. Before joining his father's operation twenty years ago, Kim, an economics graduate from Brandeis, gave the Korean skiing industry a kick-start by establishing his own resort, as if to demonstrate that his achievements could not be put down solely to nepotism.

The new taipan in charge of Samsung is Lee Kun-Hee, still only

29

forty-nine years old. Lee, the third son of Lee Byung Chull, is on record as believing that in today's world, pre-eminence is the only secret to survival. It is not enough for him to make Samsung, which was founded in 1938 as a general trading company, one of the very best in Korea. He is only interested in being among the best in the world.

Samsung is well known for its manufacture and assembly of fax machines, microwave ovens and televisions, but these days it is also involved in production at the very highest level of modern technology, with a billion-dollar-a-year investment in semiconductors, biotechnology pharmaceuticals and colour film production. Its own chip manufacture began only nine years ago, but in that time it has come a long way from the simple assembly of foreign-made components. The company is also engaged in the more mundane production of paper and food, and operations now include some forty different corporate entities.

One of the younger 'chaebols', at barely thirty years old, is Daewoo, which is making great international inroads of late into Eastern Europe and the countries of the Russian Federation. The company, which started out in the export of textiles, is today still headed by its founder, Kim Woo-Choong. It is now involved in oil production in Belgium, tyre manufacture in the Sudan, and the manufacture and distribution of cars, heavy machinery and electronics. Daewoo ships to countries all over the world, often taking payment in kind from those countries where hard currency is a problem. A self-confessed workaholic, Kim needs little sleep, and is averse to taking time off.

Another Korean company, Lucky-Goldstar, a family-controlled electronics and petrochemical trading conglomerate, is also making great strides in expanding overseas, with the manufacture of microwaves in Britain, fridges in Italy, and TVs and VCRs in Germany.

The reasons why these new taipans and their companies have been able to grow and flourish are simple. From the very beginning there was an ample supply of willing labour, and adequate capital at each stage to allow further growth. The emphasis on education and investment in skills training has meant that the workforce has been able to keep up with the continually changing demands made on it. Most important of all is that *je ne sais quoi* which to date the rest of the world has been unable to reproduce. It can be summed up by saying that so far no Asian worker has been diagnosed as suffering from attention deficit disorder. According to *The Economist*, even if Latin America and Africa were to invest as much in machines and people as East Asia, they still could not match the Asian achievement. Their combined per annum rate of capital and labour productivity growth over the last twenty years would only be about 1% compared with East Asia's 4%.

The inescapable fact that these conglomerates continue to burgeon even in a time of world recession requires a more complex explanation. Later in this book, attempts will be made to 'mind-map' the new taipans – that is, to try to understand why they do what they do, in an area-by-area breakdown of these businessmen and their domains.

Chapter 4

Heaven is High and the Emperor is Far Away

There is little mystery in the new taipans' ability to succeed at the highest levels of commercial enterprise. Neither, however, is there any surefire formula. If there is a key ingredient it seems to be dogged practicality and common sense in all areas of business, applied from the top down. Taipans are nothing if not thoroughly autocratic.

None of the taipans seems keen to admit that he set out to be a megastar of the commercial world. A public ego, where it is apparent, is usually an afterthought once success has been achieved. Hong Kong's Dickson Poon, of Dickson Concepts, one of the largest dealers of luxury goods, appeared in lavish media coverage early on in his career. These days his exposure is considerably less, and he has reverted to a public persona that is perhaps closer to his rather shy and charming self. Most of his peers would consider any form of publicity seeking an undesirable personal weakness. Acclaim must be won or earned, but not consciously sought. For this reason there is very little material available in print about any of the new taipans, and the level of familiarity in the West with either their personalities or their achievements is still negligible.

With hindsight, it is perfectly clear when studying the new taipans that empires were being built every step of the way, a fact that serves to illuminate the firmness of their business resolve. The taipans believe strongly that only doing a job properly and following a logical course to its ultimate end will lead to undreamed-of success.

There is real aggression in the business dealings of the new taipans, especially in comparison with the ponderous boardroom rituals common in Europe and America. The scale of entrepreneurship is formidable: a deal is always on the table. Taking time to explore possibilities is considered wasteful. Pragmatism is a greater virtue than strict commercial legality. That is not to say that laws are broken: they are bent and worked with – a subtle difference. Risk-taking is at a level that Western businessmen would consider fool-hardy. Decision-making and the ability to smell a profit are para-mount. Cash flow is always emphasised over the accounting precision of profit and loss.

The majority of the new taipans, throughout the Asian-Pacific region, are of Chinese origin, mainly from Guangdong province, next door to Hong Kong, and from Fujian, across the water from Taiwan. There is also something about Shanghai that seems to have encouraged a great wave of entrepreneurship.

The human resources available to these people we loosely call 'Chinese' (although they are, strictly speaking, not all of one precise race) are formidable. There is a pool of fifty-five million overseas Chinese (including twenty-one million in Taiwan and six million in Hong Kong) spread throughout twelve or so Asian countries. The business networks formed by the overseas Chinese give them con-tacts everywhere, most notably on the mainland. The real strength of this group can be measured in an estimate of their imaginary combined GNP. At approximately $450 billion, if Hong Kong and Taiwan are included, the total economic clout in question is very nearly equal to that of such countries as Israel and Spain, not a force to be ignored.

Only about thirty years ago, the flavour of life and business in Taiwan was exactly the same as that of any provincial capital on the mainland. Since then the island's tiny population has accumulated bank deposits estimated at more than $300 billion, and foreign exchange reserves of $83 billion, the largest in the world. In spite of having to maintain a large military establishment. The country's university population has also increased fifteenfold to more than 600,000 students. With a population one-third the size of that of the UK, Taiwan actually has more engineering graduates than Britain every year. And all of this before the unofficial money that floats around in a Chinese community is taken into account.

Throughout the Chinese diaspora – including North America and other more remote outposts – there is a single informal market for capital. This transnational Chinese economy already rivals Japan as a business influence. For ethnic Chinese in the Asian-Pacific Rim, the 'borderless economy' was a reality long before multinationals talked about globalisation. Collectively, the investment flow of overseas Chinese in East Asia is larger than that of the Japanese and will continue to provide the foundation for the new taipans.

Through these connections, the new taipans are almost always financially self-sufficient for new ventures. Closer inspection shows that those originating from Chiu Chow tend to deal more often with others from the same region; Hakka deals with Hakka; while the Shanghainese can be quite superior about dealing only with those from Shanghai. This approach is unimaginable to Europeans or Americans, very few of whom are familiar with large numbers of people from their own town or village. The high volume of business that takes place between the overseas Chinese and the mainland is invariably channelled through their networks of personal connections. Some 80% of Hong Kong's investments have been pouring into Guangdong province, almost equal to the percentage of Hong Kong people with relatives there. The money flowing into Fujian province comes largely from Taiwan, even though, politically speaking, there is supposedly no love lost between that island and the mainland. Overseas Chinese account for 70% to 75% of all foreign investment in China.

Non-Chinese investors, especially those Western and Japanese firms who are seriously targeting China as an investment opportunity, find it difficult to compete. The extensive networks are an unequalled business asset which, it is said, allows the overseas Chinese returns four times greater than those they might make elsewhere in Asia. The only comparable situation is that of the new maharajahs, who have the potential for a network involving the estimated eleven million overseas Indians.

Towards the end of the millennium, the world's economy will be divided roughly equally between Asian-Pacific, Europe, North America and the rest of the world. Largely because of this Chinese connection, the Asian-Pacific area will undoubtedly be the most dynamic. Indeed, the energy of the region is irresistible. The taipans know for the most part that no matter where they might find themselves living, they can start with a simple business and expand through hard work and consistency. The complexion of the local political regime, while often a major nuisance, cannot override their firm belief that discipline, economic success and continuous growth will gradually lead to greater political freedom. They also know something that the West often finds hard to accept: that if political freedom and democracy must come first, above all other priorities, satisfactory economic growth may never be achieved.

The new taipans always work with long-established business connections anywhere they choose, as opposed to the typical European or American company which generally assigns responsibilities based on national boundaries. The possibilities are endless, since ethnic Chinese are in the majority in Hong Kong, Singapore and Taiwan, and dominate the non-government economic sector in Malaysia, Thailand and Indonesia.

The taipans rarely use financial institutions for business loans. This freedom is possible because of the percentage of the overseas Chinese income that is put directly into savings of one sort or another. In many of the Asian-Pacific countries, as much as one-third of the national income is saved. The assets of the fifty-five million overseas Chinese worldwide are estimated at $2 trillion, roughly the same as those of the Japanese, who have a population twice the size.

A Chinese writer once compared his native culture to a tray of sand in which each grain represents one family. The families are bonded together by a sense of cohesion based on business and family loyalties, personal friendships and trust. Suspicious of government, taxes and politics, the Chinese rely on the subtleties of kinship or a common origin in a clan or village as a sound basis for both business and financing. Capital for business comes primarily from friends and acquaintances rather than institutions. The same writer likened Japanese society to a block of granite bound only by a blind sense of duty and patriotic obligation to the emperor. The emperor, clearly, does not make personal bank loans.

The Chinese emphasis on saving can be attributed to the need to be prepared for all contingencies in business, politics and personal life. For the same reason, it is common to see ragged street hawkers in Hong Kong, for example, wearing solid gold Rolexes on their wrists. The rationale is that in an emergency the watch can be traded for a large sum of cash which will provide shelter or supplies or means of escape. This attitude is easily understood when one remembers the mass emigration following the rise of Communism in 1949, when many people fled with only the clothes on their backs. Most people in Hong Kong suspect that they might have to leave their home one day with only what they can carry. Apart from one lump-sum investment in a redeemable asset, everything else is put into cash. This is deposited not into Western banks, but with groups of other investors to garner a higher-than-average return. Not for the Chinese the safe investments of mutual funds or government bonds. These are generally not considered rewarding enough.

The history of the new taipans and their peers in the diaspora has not been an easy one. There are documented reports of three hundred years of persecution, victimisation and even mass execution in exile. Natives of the adopted homelands have often been suspicious, questioning the loyalty of the immigrants even when cultural assimilation has appeared almost seamless. How can a country as large and as powerful as China, they wonder, have released its emotional grip on so many of its subjects? Locally, the immigrants are often made scapegoats for economic woes and regarded with suspicion politically. As a result, any energy that might, without such distrust, have been channelled into politics has been saved for pure business. A cohesion has formed between the overseas Chinese which, without the antagonism of the natives, might have been more temporary than the unbreakable bonds that actually exist.

To begin with, virtually the only Chinese in the Asian-Pacific area were itinerant salesmen and traders, hawking their wares wherever they could. Even then, though, there were some economic refugees in search of a better life who did settle away from their home provinces of Guangdong or Fujian. However, the sheer numbers of the overseas Chinese, coupled with the might of the mainland, has meant that persecution in new communities has often reached terrifying heights. Over the past six hundred years, migrants from China have been forced to settle under often hostile conditions. In the Philippines, the ruling Spanish confined the Chinese to an area outside Manila's city walls. The arrival in 1603 of three mainlanders rumoured to be envoys of the Ming emperor sparked riots in which 25,000 Chinese are said to have been killed.

The biggest increase in numbers came in the eighteenth century. Despite the fact that it was a time of intense European imperialism, colonial administrators did not encourage close ties between locals and Chinese. At this time, the Chinese found themselves being used increasingly as 'compradors' or go-betweens in business, in the Philippines, Malaya, Singapore and Vietnam. King Rama V of Thailand was especially keen to stimulate the growth of the Chinese community in his country, so much so that they soon made up 10% of the population.

Uprisings, however, such as an 1848 riot in Thailand against taxes on Chinese-dominated sugar refineries, kept locals suspicious. If the immigrants became too numerous, governors found that ethnic hostilities conveniently kept populations down. Even independence from imperial rule made matters little better, as post-colonial elites came to resent the Chinese hold on the economy. In Thailand, in 1939, Plaek Pibulsongkram's government enacted several laws to contain Chinese business activities. In the early 1960s, Indonesia banned Chinese schools and publications in order to promote assimilation, a move followed by the Philippines a decade later. In the 1960s there were bloody anti-Chinese riots in Malaysia and Indonesia, with some 90,000 Chinese fleeing for their lives from Indonesia's terrorising regime.

Many Chinese have discovered that the best way to protect themselves is by making a Faustian pact of sorts with politically powerful but often commercially inept individuals or groups. This explains to a large degree why overseas Chinese, although by nature politically disinterested, have often allied themselves in joint ventures with corrupt governments or military regimes. They may not like the liaison, but if it makes money and saves lives, the solution is a practical one.

As the region races toward development, history no longer haunts the overseas Chinese. They have gained not only economic clout but political influence. Ex-Thai prime minister Chatichai Choonhavan and the Philippines' Corazon Aquino are examples of how the descendants of labourers and traders have become politically supreme. Despite mutual suspicion, the immigrants and their hosts need and complement each other. Their futures, like their pasts, are inextricably linked.

The rise of the new taipans has occurred in those countries which have enjoyed the fastest rate of growth over the past three decades. Basically it is the four 'tigers' — Taiwan, Hong Kong, Singapore and Korea — that have raised and nurtured them. Of these, only South Korea is non-Chinese, but it shares nevertheless many of the same business traits and attitudes, while multi-ethnic Singapore is dominated by the Chinese. The other countries the new taipans find themselves born into — Indonesia, Malaysia, the Philippines, Thailand and Vietnam — all have significant overseas Chinese minorities running a disproportionate share of business.

Though overseas Chinese are estimated to make up only 4% of Indonesia's population, they are said to own seventeen of the two dozen or so of that country's top business groups, and some two-thirds of all assets that are neither foreign- nor government-owned.

In Malaysia's Islamic Fundamentalist society – which might at first glance appear unsympathetic to the Chinese way of business – approximately one-third of the population is Chinese but their influence on the economy is disproportionately significant. Malaysia's prime minister, Dr Mahathir, introduced his 'bumiputra' preference programme largely to stem the very obvious Chinese economic success. The government tried for twenty years to reduce Chinese influence by forcing the transfer (often faked) of Chinese-owned company shares to Malays or 'bumis'. This policy was only recently and half-heartedly abandoned when for the first time the potential gains of business liaisons with the Chinese began to be understood.

It is difficult to detect the fact that the Chinese constitute 10% of Thailand's population of 55 million people, and as much as one-third of the population of Bangkok. Many Thai Chinese have married natives and assumed local names. Few have hung on to their old language. Local antipathy towards them, where it does exist, is easily explained as sheer envy: this small group of people owns a vast 90% of all manufacturing and commercial assets.

Whilst the economy of the Philippines is still relatively backward, and may be slow to progress, there is some potential. Any success that does occur will be largely due to Chinese efforts. Although only a tiny 1% of people in the Philippines are pure Chinese, they nevertheless dominate as much as three-quarters of the country's business. Corazon Aquino and many other Filipino notables are proud of their partially Chinese heritage.

There are very few Bill Gates', Sir Clive Sinclairs or Alan Sugars in the Asian-Pacific Rim generally, and fewer still among the new taipans. These brilliant but fanciful types, who sometimes base a mammoth profit-seeking business venture on a single, unproven idea, are little understood and even less admired. Perhaps because Asian markets are much smaller than those of the US, the scale required to become a major taipan is more easily achieved in several businesses than in a single one.

Most Asian countries accord more honour to the man who knows his proper place, waits his turn and does his duty than to the one who steps out of line. In America, those who take enormous risks are considered heroes: chance and rule-breaking are admired as embodying the true spirit of the American pioneer. For the taipans, however, there is always an awareness of the right thing to do at the right time, and a certainty that the chance will eventually come. Innovation and setting oneself apart might turn out to be an embarrassing failure. Why not let others blaze the trail, with the accompanying exorbitant costs of research, development and marketing?

Status is something that can change very quickly among the taipans. In the mid eighties, the Ma family, of the Oriental Press Group, were embarrassed by the disappearance of the family head, 'White Powder Ma', to Taiwan. Nevertheless, the Mas were sufficiently rehabilitated in the eyes of Hong Kong society that when the family matriarch died, half of EXCO, the executive ruling committee of Hong Kong, including the Chief Secretary to the government, turned out for her funeral. While there is often some residual social stigma that clings to those, for example, who made money trading with the Japanese during the occupation of Hong Kong, none of this is ever taken personally or borne in mind commercially, though it can cause a lingering wariness amongst those with long memories.

Sponsorship and largesse are not all that widespread among the taipans, except by those seeking gongs or publicity, who will make charitable donations to community projects to enhance the public's perception of their status. The late Sir Y. K. Pao, for example, had a penchant for donating swimming pools, and other taipans give money, goods and services to their home towns back in mainland China, perhaps in order to win goodwill. Whatever the reasons, cash flow is king, and money that does not produce immediate results, either directly or indirectly, is considered wasted.

Every employee in the taipans' organisations has a sense of place and proper duty, a situation which, to Western eyes, can look rather restricting. The flip side of this is that there is an almost inviolate corporate loyalty which creates cohesion and unmatched stability. People tend to want to stay with one particular company rather than joining a strange new 'family'. Giving twenty or even thirty years to one firm is considered a privilege. Each employee believes that his taipan is in some sense an 'honourable teacher' from whom a great deal can be learned. Instruction is largely hands-on, rather than theoretical lessons in business school. It is applied learning of the very best kind, bringing a sense of prestige that we rarely see in the West. Throughout the Asian region, this feeling of grateful subordination is all-pervasive.

All the new taipans are avid disciples of such plain-and-simple business exemplars as John Paul Getty, whose maxim is said to be 'to find a need and fill it'. The taipans believe that this needs to be done as well as possible, and at a price that is competitive but does not compromise the standard of service or goods involved. The more basic the need – food, clothing, housing or energy – and the better supplied it is, the more likely the retailer, distributor or consumer is to stick with the taipan and only the taipan as the key supplier. Over a number of years, sometimes decades, the continuity of this single strand of supply-and-demand translates into a vital building block on a larger commercial stage.

An example of this progress is Indonesian taipan Eka Tijpta Widjaja, who started out dealing in scrap metal before moving on after a considerable period of consolidation to the paper and then the palm oil businesses. His original heaps of junk have today led to the mighty Sinar Mas Group, Indonesia's second largest conglomerate. The Acer company of Taiwan and Johnson Electric of Hong Kong both started out by cloning cheap IBM-compatible machines for the bulk-buying market, establishing crucial relationships along the way before launching their own products. Malaysia's Robert Kuok Khoon Ean, now better known for the world-class Shangri-la Hotel chain, began as a sugar-cane cultivator in 1968, not seriously diversifying until 1984.

Regardless of the goods or services sold, the cost-versus-quality factor is crucial. The taipans seek to establish a toehold in the market at the expense of all possible future competition. The American accusation that Asian companies often sell substandard products to win an initial edge, however, is unfounded. The Japanese have been guilty of this dubious practice, particularly with the entry of that country's videocassette recorders into the US market. The taipans, though, know that such a policy makes no sense: they would only lose the greater market share to be won further down the road, and the transition from cheap back up to luxury, with value for money, is never an easy one. Each taipan, in his progress towards his first million-dollar turnover, concentrates on a staple item or service. His ambition is to ensure that the core business is an essential component of as many other businesses in the community as possible. The taipan is, then, a *sine qua non* of the community itself.

Thus another thread is woven into the network that links individuals and businesses to the taipan. The connections are forged for a lifetime, formed through business and strengthened by the resulting loyalty and maybe, though not necessarily, friendship. These 'guanxi' are the time-honoured means of creating ties wherever there are two or more Chinese gathered together for business purposes. It is not the same as the card-collecting habit of the North American yuppie, but is rather a practical tapestry of associated businesses bound together by a series of interlinked activities.

Now that China itself, through a programme of widespread privatisation, is waking from its previous Communist commercial dormancy, more opportunities are arising for business connections than any Chinese ever dared to dream of. Chinese officials at the highest levels, including the mayors of major cities, are encouraging, and themselves becoming deeply involved with, foreign investment and the development of joint ventures. They are working especially hard to forge links with companies offering telecommunications products and services, oil drilling equipment, agricultural machinery and computer components. As a result, more and more entrepreneurs, including non-Chinese, are now seeking to understand, imitate and involve themselves in this networking process which, while entirely natural to a Chinese, often seems alien to a 'gweilo'.

The Chinese market is everything any entrepreneur could wish for. For the new taipans, though, it is also a homecoming which they treat with a mixture of hope and caution. Although China holds bad memories for many of them, there is no getting away from the kinship and cultural ties involved, as well as the sense of duty. There is too a solid commercial reason for trading with the new, non-Communist mainland: business there is proving to be the very best anywhere in the world, creating an almost unprecedented boom. Over the past ten years, China has enjoyed one of the fastest ever rates of economic growth.

For many new taipans, involvement in the mainland began with a sort of benevolent paternalism. Seeming almost guilty about their overseas success, they donated schools, universities, medical facilities and other community projects to their own or their ancestors' birthplaces. Li Ka-Shing, for example, is involved in Shantao in the construction of three power plants and a bay bridge, as well as the establishment of a university, all schemes that would not necessarily make standard business sense. This sense of a duty to China as the motherland was fostered and encouraged by Deng Xiao Ping who clearly never underestimated the lure of his new money-making machine. After the start of China's economic reforms in 1979, the mainland developed close ties with ethnic Chinese business leaders in other countries in the region, particularly Hong Kong, Taiwan and the ASEAN members. Today the money, the managers and the export know-how from those specifically targeted countries are spearheading China's economic and industrial development. Japan may be China's biggest provider of foreign loans, but two-thirds of the flood of direct overseas investment – about $15 billion a year – comes from sources in Hong Kong and Taiwan, while overseas Chinese in the rest of Asia bring in as much as another fifth of the total.

As we have seen, every business discussed in this book began as a one-man, one-product operation, which means that autocracy is a key element. No consensus is required or sought and no disagreement allowed for. Some would dub the taipans' business style 'wheeler-dealing' – a great deal of negotiation and discussion for a large number of small deals which then grow into ever-larger transactions. The Chinese are very good at dealing. Virgin's Richard Branson has expressed a preference for Chinese accountants because they have an uncanny knack with money and an innate feeling for the right price to pay. An acute sense of timing and a gift for being in the right place and charging the right price are instinctive in all the taipans, abilities which are invaluable in their traditional businesses of property and the trading of commodities.

The biggest advantage for the taipans of a one-man operation is that decision-making and responses are nearly always instantaneous, allowing for the best possible reactions to changing markets. There is no waiting around for boardroom decisions, no dissatisfied customers moving on elsewhere in their impatience. The business runs smoothly along a single track until the autocrat decides otherwise. This is only when diversification into new areas of business will bring minimal disruption.

The autocratic decision-making process and lack of formal management structure work very well until the question of succession arises. If a son or other close relative fails to make the grade, there is no hierarchy of non-family managers to fall back on. The problem has been a thorny one for a number of Thai families (as discussed in Chapter 3) and has in some cases led to the virtual destruction of the corporation. In the past, a candidate has always had to be a member of the family to be considered worthy of succession to the highest executive position. It would be unthinkable for the family to own less than a 35 to 40% share in their own company, and it is therefore imperative that those who stand to inherit also be involved in its management.

Nevertheless, more and more ethnic Chinese enterprises are today listing on stock exchanges and bringing in professional managers. One example of an outside manager is Englishman Simon Murray, who was until recently Li Ka-Shing's most trusted aide. Murray admits, though, that Li never allowed him anything approaching autonomy during his time at Hutchison Whampoa.

In a study of companies listed on the various stock markets of the region, nothing is as it seems. Identifying who owns what, and where, is a major undertaking, clouded by asset secrets such as nominee-held shares. As a rule, families work on the principle that nothing is more important than absolute and undiluted control. Responsibility for running the firm is handed down through the generations, and it is considered a duty and an honour to discharge those corporate responsibilities. Many are the fully trained and established dentists or doctors who have had to return to Asia from the United States or Australia to pick up the reins when the family head dies or retires.

The balance between money and values is always an interesting subject, and Asia is no exception. Throughout Chinese, Japanese and Korean society, teachers and doctors enjoy great respect, yet earn disproportionately small salaries. The quid pro quo is social status, which entices rather more talent into the medical and teaching professions than might otherwise be tempted.

Defining Confucianism is almost as difficult as explaining the concept of 'face', but it is perhaps best understood in terms of the tenets and abilities it inculcates. The teaching process of Confucian societies involves a great deal of rigid discipline and learning by rote, with little emphasis on personal achievement, creativity or intellectual gymnastics. The system instils in the pupil the notion that his role is not an individual one but that he is part of a great whole where quick-wittedness, dependability and constancy are paramount. There is a sense that the job you end up with is the one you were meant to have, and therefore you must give it your all. Second-best does not exist as a concept. The overriding value –

above even money and ethics – is always the family. They must come first in everything.

The family nature of the taipans' businesses, however, does not prevent them from growing into serious giants. In Indonesia, for example, just one family, that of Liem Sioe Liong, accounts for 5% of the entire country's GDP. Conglomerates are burgeoning all over South-East Asia – in Taiwan and Hong Kong particularly – creating more billionaires each year. The late Sir Y. K. Pao, the shipping and property magnate, decided to carve up his corporate empire amongst his family. The spoils were distributed to his sons-in-law, who happened to be a Japanese architect, a Shanghai-descended Hong Kong businessman, an Austrian businessman, and a Singaporean-Chinese doctor. Pao felt that in this way his own flesh and blood would at least vicariously, through their spouses, still be in control. The results have been extraordinarily beneficial: a joint venture with the Virgin Retail Group to form Virgin Megastores (HK) Ltd; the opening of a corporate office in Shanghai to provide a China base; an agreement with Foster's, the brewers, to explore Chinese brewing potential; and a joint venture with National Westminster Bank to provide stockbroking, corporate finance and investment management services. Achieving such diversification within a two-year period would have been a lot harder without 'guanxi'. Even though a taipan's company may from the outside look as institutionalised as any large Western business, there are always those family or birthplace connections available to call on.

The extraordinary success of the last decade or so has caused several taipans to embark on the formation of a new network based on the profusion of second-generation Chinese MBAs. Educated abroad, in the United States, Australia and Britain, these young Chinese have their own 'guanxi', underpinned by their fellow alumni. In this way, new thinking and practices have been introduced into the time-honoured Chinese business philosophy, to remarkable effect. Li Ka-Shing, perhaps in canny anticipation of this trend, sent both his sons to Stanford, where between them they have gained a number of degrees. This is said to have had a profound influence on the types of businesses that their father has allowed them to run, as well as on the way they have managed those enterprises. No longer do areas outside the traditional Chinese business province seem quite so daunting and impenetrable. The combination of the family-first concept and the diversified new influences acquired from a foreign education has created a fresh business dynamic. Nevertheless, the fundamental reasons for success may remain the same. New methods and philosophies often serve only to confirm that the old ways, the Chinese ways, are best.

These 'Chinese ways' are based on a hard core of philosophy, drawn from a number of sources. A brief discussion of that philosophy will help in understanding what makes the taipans act in the way they do. There are three main Chinese religions from which the taipans draw their ideas: Confucianism, Taoism, and Buddhism. The best Chinese businessmen are a little of each. Confucianism is not really a religion except in that every great religion has an ideology with a framework of superstitions, dogmas, rituals and institutions. Almost all Chinese businessmen are attached to the traditional wind and water divination rite known as 'feng shui', and to its application in business, and most still consult their human oracle on everything from stock acquisition to the siting of a new office or factory.

It is a basic truth, they would argue, that every man should engage in systematic reflective thinking about his actions and his purpose. Actions without careful thought can only lead to trouble. The Chinese are not a people consumed with religion but they are obsessed with 'face', and that is the basis of the application of Confucian ethics in daily life. They are of course conscious of higher values too: for example, the love of a god. That god may not be a Christian or even a Buddhist one, rather an indefinable almighty to whom they are accountable. They also recognise a craving for something beyond the present earthly life, one of the innate desires of mankind. It is important to them how they will be judged when they are gone, and so they give much thought to posterity.

The main purpose of Chinese philosophy, whether in an individual's business or personal life, is to increase positive and above all useful knowledge. A common bond amongst the new taipans is a desire to reach out through their business achievements beyond the present world, for those higher values. The legacy of a business – and therefore the family continuity in the business – is consequently just as important as the business itself.

Traditional Chinese thinking is said to be based on just four books – the Confucian *Analects*, the *Book of Mencius*, the *Great Learning* and the *Doctrine of the Mean* – in which no mention is made of creation or of heaven and hell. In the old days, if a man were educated at all, the first lesson he received was in philosophy. Young children studied the *Three Characters Classic*, in which each sentence consisted of three characters arranged mnemonically with a rhythmic effect, to make them more easily memorised. The very first statement to be learned was: 'The nature of man is originally good.' This goes some way to explaining why there is seldom suspicion or mistrust between the taipans.

Discrimination, whether racial, intellectual or sexual, is not regarded by the Chinese as necessarily evil, either in business or in society at large. The Western attitude, based on Christian teaching, is that prejudice is bad and should be condemned as a self-indulgent vice. It is a basic tenet in the West that all men are equal and deserve to be treated with the same respect. The cohesion of the United States, particularly, has been forged along these lines: no matter where you come from or what colour your skin is, you are an American. These ideas are not rejected outright in Asia, but are certainly not actively promoted.

Few outsiders seem aware of the racial diversity that exists within China, and the Chinese themselves always emphasise the theme of village or town, rather than that of racial origin. South Korea, which looks for all the world like a nation of 'one race, one people', in fact has deep regional divides along differing ethnic lines. The differences are barely noticeable to outsiders, but the Koreans themselves are very aware of them. Because the racial dissimilarities are hard to overcome, people in Asian countries tend to rely on national bonding to help them stick together. There is still a sense of territory and of tribal link, but this device allows different ethnic groups to work alongside each other. Lee Kuan Yew's Singapore is a shining example of national triumph in the face of extreme ethnic diversity. Each Indian, Malay and Chinese considers himself equally Singaporean. Diversity is consciously put to good use as an asset, rather than a source of disunion.

The West's Protestant work ethic has been matched in modern times by the Asian or Confucian work ethic, though there is a subtle difference between the two. The Protestant work ethic is considered to be based on the essential dignity of man. Thus, if all a man has for certain is his human dignity – if there are no guarantees for life or reward after death – it is better to work nobly than to die poor. This depends, of course, on whether there is any possibility of choice. With the welfare systems instituted on a comparatively wide scale throughout Europe, certainly for the last hundred years, there is an option. In Asia there is none. All responsibility is thrown back on to the family unit. Unmarried daughters and sons often still live at home well into their late twenties, and often work with their parents as well. The family is a survival group against the rest of the world, rather than something to be tolerated until we move on and make our own nest.

There is a constant reminder at the back of each taipan's mind that he too must work or die. Standing still for just one moment can lead to the loss of everything gained so far. Complacency is rare. This is more true now than ever, given that many businesses have been built on the back of export-led growth. With fluctuating currencies and world recession, times are tougher, and there is still no substitute for continued hard work. There is little subsidised housing or access to state aid, so people co-opt themselves into the workforce, with as much education as they can possibly get, and climb as quickly as they can to the highest possible level. They save all the way, putting money aside for the purchase of basics, for new business opportunities, and, most importantly, for education. As soon as they reach one level, they consolidate and move on higher. There is very little middle-management arrogance or smugness in Asia: a middle manager is not a taipan.

An important management consideration for the taipans is the constant threat to commercial stability. Contingency planning for an oil crisis, for a commodity shortage of one kind or another, for a natural disaster or military upset is ever present and has always been a high priority. In this way, potential pitfalls become incentives not disincentives. Where in the West a 'why bother?' attitude might prevail in adversity, the taipans' approach is 'why not?'. For example, there is every confidence among them that Hong Kong will survive, in one form or another, as an important business centre after 1997, because their contingency planning has always allowed for the possibility that the worst might happen. Deals will continue to be done and money will continue to be made, though not necessarily in the same ways as now. Every country in the region continually faces some potentially dire threat or another which merely keeps business-men, if not politicians, on their toes.

The taipans' empires are run along similar lines to each other. A typical company, with a turnover of perhaps $100 million or more a year, may operate on several continents at any one time. It may also deal with an enormous variety of products, originating from factories all around the world. Money and assets are often spread among a dozen different territories. Most companies finance their operations exclusively from cash flow, and except for the largest companies and conglomerates, there is often no corporate headquarters or chief financial officer. Sometimes there is no clearly identifiable chain of command. In business dealings, a request for a business card will often result in the production of a variety of cards, all with different company names and positions on them. No one does just one job at one time, but a little bit of everything at the same time. As for the board of directors, their position is often nominal rather than executive. Everyone in the corporation is a generalist, and if there are corporate divisions, the walls between them are more than usually fluid.

Over a period of one or two generations, the firm will have faced a number of crises — economic depression, war, persecution or earthquake — and will have survived, learned and moved on. Setbacks are perceived as beneficial in that they teach the company lessons for the future and help to mature the corporate philosophy. Competition is regarded as an opportunity to improve products for the marketplace and to achieve a visible presence for the company.

There is an ad running in Asia at the moment with a headline which reads: 'This man is the chef, the chauffeur, and the chief executive. In short, an entrepreneur.' The picture below portrays a fairly typical street hawker astride his bicycle food cart, waiting to sell his noodles to passers-by. 'Businessmen in Asia,' the text continues, 'rarely stand still. If there's an opportunity round the corner they'll take it.' That advertisement sums up the attitude of the taipans. Most have built themselves up from itinerant traders to become highly respected and influential business leaders. The key traits are patience, cunning and complete control over every facet of operations. The taipan's personal philosophy dominates his company, from the lowest clerical level to the million-dollar export deal.

Many taipans who were born in China were brought up elsewhere in the region and may have worked for relatives in several cities. They will have started out with whatever job was on offer from the family, being careful to learn and to contribute as much as possible. From involvement in a family operation, the embryonic taipan learns the importance of keeping control in the hands of as few trusted family members as possible.

At some stage the taipan will have decided that he has had enough 'training' to establish a business of his own, but always, as discussed, in a simple supply-based operation and not on projected demand. Frequently he will have started one or two complementary businesses, concluding that if he is destined to be a success, it might as well be twofold. It is in this first enterprise that key connections are made, without which future success is all but impossible. If new territories and bases for operation and production are to be explored, building up a network is invaluable. Sometimes a degree of assimilation has been required by this stage in order to foster a local presence and sense of belonging. This may be achieved by a change of name, a venture with someone in the indigenous community, or marriage.

Only if the circumstances allow it will the taipan have developed political as well as business connections. He would consider most involvement in politics to be a great deal more trouble than it is ever likely to be worth. The recently generated business with a revitalised China is fraught with political problems. Trying to sell products and services to both Taiwan and the mainland, for example, throws up a nightmare of Kuomintang versus Communist allegiances. All have to be carefully side-stepped.

When one family spreads throughout the diaspora, they learn the local cultures and languages en route and constantly add more contacts to the network. In this way, they gain access to critical market information and new business opportunities that would normally only be available to vast multinational corporations. This same process through the more orthodox means of hired market intelligence would cost many tens of thousands of dollars.

Juggling a number of commercial balls in several different places has the added advantage that if one important business contact should fall hopelessly by the wayside, there will always be another somewhere else. For this reason, top Hong Kong businessmen started cultivating operations in places such as Bangkok, Singapore and Vietnam well before 1997 was an issue. In lean times, even businessmen who have had substantial operations have been known to move back down the hierarchy to set up a small shop that will at least provide a subsistence living. Stanley Ho, of Macau hydrofoil and casino fame, has won and lost fortunes several times over the years. With time and patience, even the most humble of businesses presents an opportunity to expand and regain status.

The cleverest of taipans will always go the extra mile in doing a deal. If buying a commodity in, say, China, they will often make a special effort to arrange the best prices for the producer, and will also insist on developing further strands of the business. They may institute educational and training programmes, or introduce new technology and technical assistance, thus establishing a long-term alliance. A taipan tries to think from the producer's point of view, not just out of altruism but with the very sharpest commercial intent. When it becomes clear that the taipan is not just looking to make a quick buck, the relationship will be cemented in a respect and friendship that should last for years. Personal incomes palpably improve as a result of this relationship, contributing to an atmosphere of stability and trust. This sort of value-added approach would be considered far too generous by those accustomed to the Western style of business.

Sooner or later, one of the offspring of the new taipans finds that he is able to take advantage of the prosperity of the family business to go to an American, Australian or European university, where, given the innate Asian work ethic, he or she usually excels. Sometimes the first instinct of this second generation is to imagine that perhaps they could do better outside the family business. Familiarity has bred complacency. But after some training elsewhere, picking up skills that are always useful, they realise the commercial advantages of becoming a prodigal son or daughter. They will never have to start from scratch as their father or grandfather did before them. From their unique position, they are free to consolidate, expand and build on the empire.

As the world has changed, the usefulness of the taipan as a mere middleman has diminished, forcing him to reconsider the *raison d'être* of his business. One of the main guarantees of success for the taipans has always been their indispensability to their customers. As this can no longer be assured, new areas have had to be explored. Expertise in accountancy and management has led many taipans into the areas of computing, technology and telecommunications. Whatever field they go into, that same network of contacts can be brought into play once again, this time for the purpose of marketing an end product. Nowadays, even relatives who were cut off by the revolution in 1949 are joining the family company. Those who endured the Cultural Revolution in the 1960s seem particularly keen to succeed as 'capitalist pig' businessmen.

With the initial opening in China's Bamboo Curtain after President Nixon's 1972 visit to Beijing, a fountain of commercial opportunity sprang up. The Canton Trade Fair provided one of the first real exchanges of business between the Communist and non-Communist divisions of many families. No opportunity was left unexplored. Most of what we witness today found its roots in that opening more than twenty years ago. Some observers believe that recent developments in China, such as new taxes on the 'excess profits' of privately owned companies, are a sign that the good times will not last. It could be that orthodox Marxism has never really been killed and that the vicious Phoenix of communism will rise again.

Nothing, though, will surprise the taipans. They have seen it all before and know very well that they can cope.

Chapter 5

An Acute Case of Growing Pains

A study of the new taipans in their present form might lead the casual observer to believe that the road to riches and commercial fame has always been an easy one. According to an article by William Mellor in the magazine *Asia Inc.*, the world's first trillionaire will be Asian. Among the candidates most likely to achieve this financial distinction are Hong Kong's Lee Shau-Kee, the Kwok brothers of Sun Hung Kai, Li Ka-Shing, Robert Ng, and Robert Kuok; Taiwan's Tsai Hungtu, and Y. C. Wang; Indonesia's Liem Sioe Liong and Eka Tijpta Widjaja; and Korea's Shin Kyuk-Ho, Chung Ju-Young, and Lee Kun-Hee. Of these, the first past the post is likely to be Lee Shau-Kee, who is estimated to need growth of only 20% for another twenty-seven years in order to amass a fortune of $1 trillion. Even with a growth rate of only 10% per annum, which would be unusually low for Lee, he would make his first trillion in just fifty-two years. In the past, conditions have been far less amenable to growth than they are now. The seventies and eighties were a testing ground for commercial skills.

The money tree these magnates have planted is well fertilised, not by good fortune but by the study and practical implementation of philosophies found in classical and ancient Chinese literature. These philosophies are never more important than in the lean times. Most Asian companies, at some point during their history, have triumphed over volatile economic and political conditions at home, fierce competition in local regional markets and rising protectionist sentiment and continued recession in the West. Many businessmen in Asia include in their management strategies such tenets as 'Launch an attack when it is least expected'; 'Strong and weak can be reversed'; 'Know yourself and your enemy'.

Chinese businessmen now note, with not a little amusement, that the most faithful followers of this commercial ideology to date have been the Japanese, whose companies have applied the acquired philosophies with almost religious fervour. Indeed, this school of thought is widely, if erroneously, known as the 'Japanese style of business'.

The greatest growing pain that all the countries of the Asian-Pacific region have had to deal with is shaking off the image that the West had of them as a source of cheap labour and materials to be exploited by overseas expertise. The radical change in the West's perception of Asia's potential came at a time when it would have been much easier for the area to simply continue as a convenient sweatshop until the problems of recession had diminished. Instead, a bolder stance was taken.

For Hong Kong, grappling with the issue of 1997 and the future of the colony presented additional problems. Some businessmen, like Shanghai-born Peter Woo of World and Wharf Holdings, attacked the dilemma head-on. His company published *The Challenge of Hong Kong Plus*, a book designed to position Hong Kong, and therefore World itself, as a fulcrum for investors to take advantage of the Greater China market. The book was published at a time when all around him were underplaying the importance of Hong Kong in the future of the region.

There have been so many problems in the countries of the Asian-Pacific generally that at one time their very economic survival, let alone the rampant economic growth they have in fact enjoyed, seemed impossible. Throughout the 1970s and 1980s, most of the countries concerned suffered a degree of domestic political unrest that would have caused many companies elsewhere in the world to throw up barricades and down tools in alarm.

Abroad, there was a different kind of problem to be dealt with, that of rising protectionism. Just as Asia was getting into the swing of easy, large-scale competitive production, down came the world's gates to thwart its economic progress. One way of surmounting the difficulties was through government backing. In Korea, for example, the 'chaebols' were able to orchestrate campaigns at the highest level to lobby and persuade the government, a strategy which eventually showed results. Singapore followed suit, and was able to offer favourable offshore bases in the Pacific Rim to American, Australian and European companies. Joint ventures, not necessarily favourable to the

Asian companies concerned, were undertaken as a sign of goodwill. Appeasement was an important weapon in the commercial battle-ground.

In the 1980s, many Asian countries which had developed nearly double-digit annual growth rates found themselves in a state of sudden shrinkage. Large numbers of people were thrown out of work as orders dwindled, and foreign investment declined sufficiently to cause alarm. These countries knew they could no longer rely on the multinationals for business. There would be no security as long as their work continued to be produced piecemeal for overseas commercial interests. From now on, they would have to look inward. Decisions were taken, at both government and corporate level, to somehow develop native conglomerates with their own technology and expertise.

Asian conglomerates generally fall into one of two categories: 'structurers' and 'builders'. The 'builders' usually focus on a core manufacturing business. Taiwan's President Enterprises and Thailand's C. P. Pokhphand, two of Asia's biggest food-based companies, are in this group. The 'structurers' are free-wheeling deal-makers, quick to exploit their connections to corner a market, irrespective of what or where it is. One example of a 'structurer' is Robert Kuok. When many other commodity kingpins were falling by the wayside in the seventies and eighties, Kuok was involved, along with many other taipans, in developing a value-added strategy that would allow companies in Hong Kong, Taiwan, Malaysia, Singapore, Indonesia, and Thailand to move from being mere collaborators to providing world competition that would beat both the Americans and the Japanese at their own game.

Risk in times of hardship provides the greatest potential for return, something of which the Riadys of the Lippo group of Hong Kong are well aware. When others have scoffed at the idea of property trading, Lippo Ltd has plunged in headlong, with spectacular results. The Riadys do exercise some caution, however: they do not buy anything unless they have someone lined up to sell on to. Their fearless approach has led them to invest heavily in China – in offices, shops, flats, hotels and a power station – mostly in their family's former home, Fujian province. They are also involved in the development of Meizhou island off Fujian, where there is a shrine popular with Taiwanese tourists. If direct trade links between Taiwan and the mainland are restored, the area will blossom.

Anxious not to be too reliant on the Japanese economy for investment, the ASEAN four – Hong Kong, South Korea, Singapore and Taiwan – began in the mid eighties a programme of mutual investment. By 1991, intra-Asian investment in the four countries, at 30%, was surpassing that of the Japanese, at only 15%. This shift was due to a number of factors. The ASEAN nations had come to realise that Japan was having troubles of its own and could not be relied upon for investment in the same way as before. The Chinese networks immediately came into play, using established links to root out new opportunities abroad. At the same time, currency surges, particularly in Korea and Taiwan, made moving offshore a necessity.

As part of the new thinking, Asian businesses would no longer be dependent on the whims of overseas buyers, but would become viable markets in their own right, if necessary for their own goods. Firms would make a giant leap into the unknown arena of product and service research and development, and then on into the market-ing and distribution of those products. The taipans used the adversity that Western problems had thrust upon them to create new oppor-tunities. Unintentionally or not, they were helped by their respective governments, who provided lower corporate taxes, venture capital funds, and low-interest loans, thereby financing the companies as they strove for independence.

Flexibility in product lines and services has allowed Asian cor-porations to mould their business to the market. The companies see themselves as management and investment holding companies rather than makers of predetermined goods. They regard their position as being one where opportunities are identified and needs met even when the resources – such as certain new technologies – are not immediately available in their own arsenal. When tried-and-trusted products begin to fail because of a fall-off in demand, companies are quick to make sometimes radical switches, something which is not often known to happen in the West.

This philosophy is applied across the board, even extending to the fashion business. In the seventies and early eighties, Asian clothes manufacturers were commonly regarded as being at the very cheapest end of the rag trade. All at once, the companies in that sector performed a volte-face. No longer would they be the purveyors of cheap and cheerful T-shirts and dresses. They would move on and up to manufacture for the great and good of New York's Seventh Avenue, hoping eventually that clothes produced in Hong Kong would have a cachet of their own. As a result, the colony has produced a stream of home-grown designers like Eddie Lau, Ragence Lam, Izabel Lam and Hannah Pang, all well known globally. The fashion crowd now flock to Hong Kong, partly to take advantage of new production techniques and also to breathe in some of the creative flair that is increasingly apparent there.

In electronics and computer technology, too, this change of emphasis from mere producer to innovator has allowed Hong Kong and other countries to develop a key group of technicians, product designers and inventors who are able to educate and train labour in China, Indonesia, and even South America. Spiralling costs in the sector have forced companies to move production offshore, a step requiring both patience and perseverance. Happily, the risk seems to have paid dividends.

In order to meet the challenges of unpredictable commercial conditions, the most successful Asian companies have taken a number of specific steps. They have without fail adopted a long-term management plan by launching into brand-new businesses, technologies and markets. They have re-invented their management style – or rather have kept it in a state of permanent flexibility – so that they can better read the marketplace and their customers. They have gradually tackled the problems of business ethics – specifically, corruption – and quality control, in order to ensure that they have a fitting reputation for the world stage. Finally, and in many cases for the first time, they are looking within to raise the morale and motivation of their employees as high as they can.

There is no question that the People's Republic of China, as a market in its own right and as a catalyst in a greater economic reaction, has been a key factor in the success stories of the taipans. The country has provided a backdrop against which some of their greatest and certainly most valuable commercial dramas have been played out. However, as recently as the early 1990s, China as a market appeared to most of the world to be nothing more than a wild commercial fantasy. Sceptics argued that the Communist system – which even now refuses to lie down and die – was completely at odds with the free market economy that serious commercial success requires. Against all the odds, and frequently with great commercial pain and financial loss, the taipans ploughed on regardless. While others argued that the country was too backward, overly bureaucratic, corrupt and greedy, they pursued their own clear goals with a steady resolve.

For many, then, the Chinese market was always something of a myth, or a long-term hope at best. Others were disillusioned by the Tiananmen Square massacre, which blasted many an incipient business initiative out of the water. The China bubble appeared to have burst. Apart from anything else, one billion people without as basic a requirement as electricity were obviously not going to buy a great many computers, hamburgers or anything else. American and European companies, many of whom had started out with a commercial bang in China, were pulling back personnel and shutting down offices. They argued that the very high rents made no sense in view of only diminishing returns. While rates of pay for local personnel were low on paper, they were boosted by 'hao cho', the bonus payments that in China go with every deal. Even though there was obviously money to be made, many Westerners argued, the monies could not be repatriated without tremendous difficulty.

The taipans, though, understood the rules of the 'buy low, sell high' commercial game, if only because they themselves were practitioners of it. Unlike many in the West, the Asians knew that as long as China was short of foreign exchange – which it would continue to be for a considerable time – they would have to accept raw commodities in exchange for goods and services. It was a huge risk, but one the taipans were happy to take: their focus was not on the immediate balance sheet but on the enormous profits to be had further down the road.

In China today, the most significant investors, as we have seen, are the overseas Chinese. The reason why their efforts have paid off is that they have shown a perseverance second to none. They have also been able to rely on their networks of personal relationships to manoeuvre through seemingly insurmountable obstacles, including political problems and world recession. They have also had to deal with interference by Chinese bureaucrats and sudden personnel changes during joint ventures.

While many American and European pioneers in China have thrown up their hands and backed away in disgust, the new taipans have waited doggedly for deals to come through. They understand and accept the so-called 'two plus two equals a half' formula: deals in China will take twice as long and cost at least twice as much as business anywhere else, and yet the return on investment is only half of the reward that could reasonably be expected elsewhere. Although that rule changes and better results eventually emerge, it is small wonder that so many non-Chinese gave up. That failure to wait and to work with different business formulae caused a large number of Western companies to lose out.

In the early 1980s Gordon Wu was regarded simply as a small-time property developer. To read about him today, it is easy to imagine that his progress to his present multi-million-dollar dealings in China, culminating in the phenomenal highway from Hong Kong to Guangdong, has been plain sailing. However, even he has had problems along the way. In 1989, after the Tiananmen Square massacre, the banks refused to come up with an $800m loan to finance the road. After a great deal of debate and persuasion, the Hongkong and Shanghai Bank agreed to the loan, aware of the boost that the road would give to southern China's economy. On the Chinese side too there were difficulties to be overcome. Wu spent more than a decade forming the right kind of business relationships and courting people of influence in order to be able to go ahead with the project. He also started a redevelopment project in Guangdong province for a rail terminus, only to have the plug pulled by a change of both policy and personnel. This was an expensive and time-consuming setback, but Wu puts it down to being just part of the problem of dealing with China. Few others would be so sanguine about such a loss.

One of Wu's main assets is an ability to disregard conventional – or Western – wisdom. When others were pulling out of China, after their initial headlong rush, he obstinately stayed put. He had given Hong Kong a taste of his inclination to pull against the tide by building his Hopewell Centre in Wanchai, the quarter of Hong Kong previously known only for Suzie Wong and a slew of sleazy bars. Deaf to all advice for caution, he threw in what seemed to many to be good money after bad, investing heavily in infrastructural project after infrastructural project with no realistic hope – by Western standards – of anything resembling a return. Foreign stockholders became increasingly alarmed. No American, Australian or European board of directors would have put up with his apparent foolhardiness.

He began his China foray with participation with others in Guangdong's China Hotel, a modest enough first enterprise. He then moved into the supply of electricity to the province, a move that was triggered by the obvious shortcomings of the power supply to the hotel. Guangdong was at that stage producing only 420 kilowatt hours (KWH) of electricity for each of its sixty million inhabitants, compared with 3,400 KWH per head in Hong Kong. Undaunted, Wu drummed up a group of co-investors under the Citibank umbrella and produced, within a very short time, a brand-new power plant to solve the electricity problem. The cost to Wu was said to be HK$150m. in equity, out of a total cost of HK$4.4 billion. Now the power plant is making his company, Hopewell Holdings, a great deal of money, and will continue to do so until the franchise with China runs out in ten years' time.

Similar thought processes are leading Wu to build yet more power stations in Guangdong, and to embark as a partner in a consortium planning a major transportation project of elevated roads and light railways for Bangkok. These schemes will undoubtedly bear more fruit: between now and the year 2000, Asia's fastest-growing economies are planning to spend over $1 trillion on building infrastructure.

Wu is just one of many to have jumped on the bandwagon. C. P. Pokhphand, for example, which was among the first companies to put a toe into China in the early 1980s, has expanded vastly in recent years and is involved in projects such as a $3 billion petrochemical plant outside Shanghai. Bangkok Land is investing $1.4 billion in three massive housing complexes in Beijing. Robert Kuok is involved in property development projects in Beijing and Shanghai worth at least half a billion dollars.

There are still growing pains, even now, associated with success, and there probably always will be. It is essential that the countries themselves, and the conglomerates and companies within them, concentrate further on financial reform and on developing their infrastructure to keep up with the pace of growth. In Korea, for instance, the biggest 'chaebols' are massively indebted: at Samsung, for example, the electronics subsidiary took on debt equal to seven times its equity in order to finance its push into semiconductors. In many cases, the technocrats, determined to preserve their own power, prevent attempts at financial reform, so that companies have no choice but to continue to call upon informal financing for growth.

Nevertheless, there are important lessons for Western companies in the way Asia has overcome adversity. Recent breakthroughs have come about largely through diligence and hard work in all areas of business; and above all through enthusiasm. There is a new zeal in Asia that even the worst balance sheet or economic disaster cannot dampen.

Chapter 6

The Deal-Makers Go on a Binge

Once upon a time, when fear of the prospects of 1997 caused the first new migrants from Hong Kong to leave, they were considered 'boat people'. Today they are 'yacht people'. For the last few years they have been spilling into and buying up the very best areas of Sydney, Auckland, Toronto, Seattle and other major cities. Britain has not been a popular choice of destination, even though Her Majesty's Government offered ten years ago to take in a quarter of a million Hong Kong Chinese people. The two preferred countries have been Australia and Canada, each of them accepting between ten and twenty thousand people each year since 1984.

The new taipans all realise that regardless of short-term disruption, Hong Kong is likely to remain the financial and commercial centre for Greater China. Old habits and 'guanxi' are too hard to break. Although there will be some changes, business will, they believe, be able to go on in very much the same way as it does now. Hong Kong's commercial hegemony will, however, be challenged by Shanghai, and so a toehold in the People's Republic of China proper is considered essential. Australia and New Zealand are also becoming increasingly interesting as a focus for business, since these countries are going to great lengths to forge stronger economic links with Asia as a whole rather than with their old European partners.

Above all, the taipans have come to understand that it is a powerful East Asia – the industrialised belt of Japan, Korea, Taiwan, Hong Kong and coastal China – that will provide the world's most influential power base for business in the next century. Many economists have predicted that China will exceed America in total GNP by a factor of twenty in the next thirty years. Furthermore, they believe that the East Asian elites will reach incomes equivalent to the top

61

10% of Americans, and in so doing will pull the rest of their nations up by the bootstraps.

In the meantime, however, the taipans have sensibly prepared contingency plans, establishing boltholes in other countries and often moving corporate headquarters to offshore locations as a safety measure. These boltholes are also a useful base from which to expand existing operations on to a global platform. Partners in expansion are often sought amongst the American multinationals, who are rightly considered to have long been contributors to the development of the Asian region. The taipans believe that the Americans have the edge over the Japanese when it comes to doing business on a world scale. Although no one is better qualified as a partner than another overseas Chinese, the Americans are the least distrusted of foreign partners as far as the new taipans are concerned. They are also thought to be less likely to be a source of local staffing problems in any joint venture. The Japanese, on the other hand, are very reluctant to place anyone other than their own nationals in management positions, an attitude which can cause resentment.

There are a number of historical enmities which even today haunt Asians' perceptions of one another: a continuing animosity between Chinese and Japanese as a result of the Sino-Japanese War; and hostility between Vietnamese and Chinese because of the expulsion of ethnic Chinese – the boat people – from Vietnam. A particularly watchful eye is kept on the China–Japan relationship, affecting as it does the prospects for continued peace and stability in the region – a *sine qua non* of sound business development.

The third leg of the new global business relationship that the taipans have come to concentrate on – together with the overseas Chinese in Asia itself and the Chinese in mainland China – is provided by the Asian-Americans in the United States and other territories. According to recent figures, there are 7.9 million of these people – 3% of the total population of the US. In 1880, after the initial flow of immigrants, the Chinese represented only .002% of the population. About 42% of today's Asian-Americans living in metropolitan areas reside in California. Other pockets include New York City, Honolulu, and Chicago. In San Francisco, for example, there are proportionally more Chinese (15% of the city's population) than in any other major urban area in the continental United States.

The average household income of these people is notably higher than that of other American minorities, including blacks, Hispanics and American Indians. The percentage of Asian-Americans earning more than $50,000 is also higher than for any other demographic group. There are more college graduates among Asian-Americans than any other set, and a higher proportion hold professional jobs. When it comes to business ownership, they are far ahead of other population segments: 5.7% are entrepreneurs, more than double the percentage of any other minority group.

The promise for the future – both for the people themselves and for the taipans using their services – is even greater. Between 1980 and 1992, the total Asian-American population increased 123%, a much higher percentage than whites (12.5%), Hispanics (65.3%) or any other group. They are projected to number around ten million by the year 2000, or about 3.5% of the total US population.

What is especially auspicious is that enlightened businessmen are being welcomed to America in droves by the Immigration Act of 1990, which earmarked ten thousand visas for entrepreneurs with at least $1 million to put towards starting up a business. Very little further encouragement is needed for the taipans to send their sons, cousins and even aunts to open branch offices in the US. The perfect framework has unwittingly been put in place to ensure future business success. All the taipans' main criteria – of family, funding, existing business ties and familiarity – are effortlessly deployed once again, but this time on the world stage. With their 360° business vision, they cannot fail to make the best use of this situation.

The historical foundation of the structure of the Chinese community in America is not dissimilar from that of their counterparts in Australia and Canada. The original immigrants came from Hong Kong, the People's Republic of China, South-East Asia and Taiwan. An important watershed in all three territories was the collapse of the Nationalist government in China in 1949. Before that time, the émigrés were mainly working class, whereas the later wave was composed largely of highly educated professionals. The Confucian ideal maintains that one's first loyalty is to the family, so the diaspora that was created by scattering Chinese families around the world was painful to endure. Families were wrenched apart for many years, with the only reward being a good education and better prospects for future generations.

The Chinese first arrived in America in large numbers as gold prospectors, then later as sharecroppers and seasonal labourers. The discovery of gold had ignited a worldwide rush to the Sierra foothills, and the Chinese were quick to realise the potential that such a find offered: in 1852 alone, more than 20,000 of them reached 'gao gum saan' or Old Gold Mountain. They quickly established themselves in the area through hard work and perseverance, coming to be described in local press coverage of the time as 'good citizens, deserving of the respect of all'. They even had a prominent place in a San Francisco parade when California joined the Union in 1850.

In cities there were two kinds of work: doing laundry or serving in restaurants. As late as 1920, nearly a third of all Chinese Americans sweated in laundries. Most immigrants came from Guangdong province, on tickets paid for with credit against future earnings. Very few saw themselves staying permanently. All they wanted was to make a good living and to send home their earnings to their families. They went home to marry and to father children, and then returned for another spell abroad.

It was not long, however, before local feeling, born out of envy and resentment, turned against the Chinese. Of the many ugly incidents at the time, one memorable for its viciousness was in Wyoming in the mid 1880s, when Chinese who had refused to join a local miners' strike were incinerated along with their homes in an arson attack. The only reply acceptable to the immigrants was to 'bai hoi', or stand aside, so as to avoid conflict. Survival lay in always behaving as though each and every action reflected on all Chinese. Education, they reasoned, was everything. The enemy could burn down your house, but they could never take away your education. Many people are adopting a similar attitude for survival in Hong Kong after 1997.

Because of the widespread persecution of the Chinese, they tended towards insularity wherever they settled. This oppression manifested itself in many ways other than physical. Taxes were specially levied against the immigrants. The Chinese were not allowed to appear in court cases where litigation with whites was involved. Very often Chinese children were prevented from attending local schools, so the immigrants quickly established their own institutions, including newspapers, banks and other necessities. Self-reliance was paramount. There was even an all-Chinese village, Lockeport (later shortened to Locke), which was founded in 1915. Alongside its Chinese school, stores and casinos was one Caucasian-run business: a brothel.

Responding to this hostility, and in some sort of attempt to stem the tide, the US Congress eventually passed the Chinese Exclusion Act, suspending for ten years the immigration of all Chinese labourers except for students, teachers and merchants. In 1913, California went further, prohibiting the Chinese from owning land, on the grounds that they were aliens.

The Exclusion Act was finally repealed by Congress in 1943, but even then only 105 Chinese were allowed to enter the US each year. The Immigration Act of 1965 finally abolished the punitive quota system, and from 1968 China, like every other nation, was allowed 20,000 immigrants a year. In 1982 Taiwan was awarded its own separate quota. A tremendous influx of Chinese and other Asians followed.

As mentioned before, those who arrived before the 1950s were for the most part working class. Often they had relatives already living abroad, came from spartan rural backgrounds and spoke little English. Now it is the émigré professionals, and the best and brightest of the taipans' own progeny, who are turning out to be vital links in the Asian-American chain, despite the fact that they have had their roots in the New World for a relatively short time. These professionals tend to live outside concentrated Chinese communities, speak Mandarin and have assimilated rather more effortlessly.

It is said that many Asian-Americans have to work doubly hard, being 100% Asian and 100% American. The result is a commercial and cultural hybrid, adept in both worlds. Business, technology, education, the sciences and the arts are scattered with examples of the success that this endeavour and determination have brought: Chang-Lin Tien, the chancellor of the University of California, Berkeley; writers like Amy Tan (*The Joy Luck Club*) and Maxine Hong Kingston (*China Men*); the filmmaker Wayne Wang (*Dim Sum*); and Connie Chung, who co-anchors the CBS evening news with Dan Rather. Australians and North Americans now no longer expect to find Asians working solely in restaurants or laundries. They might own the business, and a few dozen others besides, but the menial task of running it is left to others.

Despite this sort of success, Asian-Americans have to face the fact that they are still regarded as foreigners in both North America and Australia, and probably always will be. Before, they had the choice of assimilating or of being alien. Now, they are trying to find their own definitions of where they belong in their new societies.

Why Asian-Americans continue to succeed, even in environments

as liberal as those of North America and Australia, is something of
a mystery. It is probably still largely attributable to a keen sense
of duty to fulfil parental expectations. There is no escape from the
Confucian idea that what you do reflects on your family.

Old political affiliations also have a bearing on the new world of
business. In both American- and Australian-Chinese communities
there has long been a divide along the lines of that on the mainland
itself. Support is either for the Nationalist Kuomintang government
based in Taiwan, favoured by the conservative elite and the American
Republican Party, or for the Communist regime of the People's
Republic of China. Those who favour the latter tend to keep quiet
on the subject, however. In today's world politics has become almost,
but not quite, incidental. Affiliations are not as important as before,
or quite so openly declared. An Australian-Chinese may freely
engage in business across partisan lines, in both Taiwan and the
PRC, without qualms of conscience or fear of reprisal. This freedom
is very useful indeed for all concerned.

But the focus of the Chinese in the new countries has anyway
always been concentrated on business rather than politics. Those
middle-class Chinese who do enter politics are more interested in
anti-discrimination legislation and Chinese representation on boards
and commissions than in basic work and housing issues. Representation heightens profiles and creates new connections and influence,
all useful in business. In the United States, there has been little
inclination even to vote, let alone stand for office, a fact borne out
by figures from the New York Chinatown Voter Education Alliance.
In 1985, for example, only 5,846 voters with Chinese surnames
were registered, out of a Chinatown population estimated to be over
100,000. The Chinese press revealed the actual voter turnout, which
was said to be a meagre 3,000 – and that was described as 'a good
year'. There has been a slight tendency amongst Chinese-Americans
to ape the vociferous and visible political activity of blacks and
Spanish-Americans. This is, however, totally out of character.

When overseas Chinese are political, they tend to vote across
party lines, believing that only fellow Chinese can fully understand
and represent them. A comparatively rare incidence of political
activity in the United States featured a group of well-known
Chinese, led by S. B. Woo and Anna Chennault, a long-time sup-
porter of the Taiwanese Nationalist government. They launched a
non-partisan campaign to pressure presidential candidates to promise

THE DEAL-MAKERS GO ON A BINGE

that, if elected, they would appoint at least three Chinese-Americans to policy-making positions. Some Asians also took part in Jesse Jackson's Rainbow Coalition in the last two presidential elections because they considered he would attract national coverage for minority issues. Such high-profile political indulgence, however, is rare.

In Vancouver, or 'Hongcouver' as it is now sometimes jokingly known, life is as different from those early pioneer days in the United States as it could be. As the nerve centre of British Columbia, the city is prosperous, with a growth rate over the past five years of 3.3%, far outstripping a much less exciting 0.7% rate of national growth. There are indeed parts of the city, with their multitude of Chinese cinemas and restaurants, that are virtually indistinguishable from Hong Kong. Vancouver's proximity to Asia, together with its favourable immigration programme – which brought assets of more than two and a half billion Canadian dollars from Asia over a five-year period – has made it a natural choice for Chinese émigrés, who now number 350,000 – 25% of the population. Even David Lam, the province's governor, is a one-time Hong Kong resident, now settled happily in Canada. Despite a natural reticence in politics, the community has nevertheless fostered sufficient political interest to produce a number of Chinese city councillors, and one MP.

Several leading Hong Kong taipans are commercially involved in Vancouver, notably the New World group's Cheng Yu-Tung, Henderson Land's Lee Shau-Kee, and Li Ka-Shing, through his company Concord Pacific Development. Li's vast property development, encompassing nearly one quarter of the city's total space, includes a business park, a commercial complex and more than 40,000 office suites.

Vancouver can boast successful new Chinese entrepreneurs in all fields of business. One of the most visible is Thomas Fung, the brother of Hong Kong-based Sun Hung Kai Securities chairman, Tony Fung. Thomas was educated in Canada and started out in a valued and much-needed business, founding the St Germain bakery chain. In classic new taipan style, he then expanded his business into the property market, and is currently working to establish what he hopes will eventually become Canada's, if not North America's, first ethnic commercial centre. Typically, Fung has filled most of the spaces in his building with a variety of his own shops and services, in order to stimulate demand.

Banks which cater to the community are also very big business.

The combined enterprise of the new émigrés has ensured that the Hongkong Bank of Canada is now the largest foreign bank in the country. The most profitable branch, not surprisingly, is that in Vancouver's Chinatown. In California, the San Francisco-based United Savings Bank, with only eighteen branches, is said to have assets of $1.3 billion and deposits of $1.1 billion, and is currently the largest US savings bank servicing the Chinese-American population. The bank divides its Chinese customers into those from Hong Kong, who are Cantonese-speaking; those from mainland China, who may speak either Cantonese or Mandarin; and those from Taiwan, who speak Mandarin. Then there are also Cantonese-speaking customers from Vietnam and a variety of others from all around the Pacific Rim. The bank's Silicon Valley branch has a large number of Taiwanese customers who tend to be businesspeople or professionals needing commercial banking, asset management and property investment services.

In the States, Shanghai-born Henry Y. Hwang, now of Los Angeles, is chairman and president of the little-known Far East National Bank. He has positioned himself perfectly to act as financier and go-between in very lucrative business deals between government parties in China, overseas Chinese businessmen all around the Pacific Rim, and US interests. There is no question that were he not Chinese-American, the opportunities would not have been open to him. Other Chinese-Americans have found themselves roles in their motherland, building hotels and apartment complexes, developing a service sector, and selling industrial equipment and high technology.

The overseas Chinese businessman most widely admired in mainland China today is the eponymous founder of Wang Laboratories, An Wang. Not only does he have a real commitment to the development of China, but he is also a very astute deal-maker. He has enjoyed considerable success in China, signing agreements to develop computer products on the mainland worth as much as $150 million per annum. His California company, TFT Inc., makes manufacturing equipment which is said to have sales in the China market worth $5 million a year. The CEO of the company, Joe Wu, was a refugee from Mao in the mid 1940s. Being Chinese gives Wu, and the thousands of others like him, distinct advantages when it comes to doing business on the mainland. Overseas Chinese are more accustomed to the primitive conditions in which they find themselves working. They will understand and accept the tiresome wheels of bureaucracy, and the eternal coffee- and tea-drinking. They are often only too willing to adapt products to local conditions rather than arguing fruitlessly about how the Chinese market will have to adjust to the ways of the West.

A major technology trade fair held recently in Beijing was attended by some two hundred entrepreneurs. Nearly all the delegates to the event, which was organised by the Asian-American Manufacturers Association, were overseas Chinese, who were able to meet and do business with potential Chinese customers and present special seminars for Chinese managers and technicians. It is through this kind of contact that the seemingly better organised and financed American giants can be soundly beaten. Foreigners cannot hope to compete with the advantage that such connections give the Chinese-Americans. Each project piggybacks on to another, and may give birth to a further commercial venture in trading, property development or the service sector. No opportunity is wasted, either at home in the States or overseas in mainland China.

The new taipans are also now able to incorporate the southern hemisphere into their global network. In recent years, the Australian government has gone out of its way to encourage Asian immigration and closer business ties with that continent. Prime Minister Paul Keating goes so far as to argue that many of Australia's economic problems are the result of its long relationship with the United Kingdom, and that all eyes must now look closer to home, to Asia. Keating has developed a plan to link the Asian and Australian economies in an integrated market of two billion people responsible for half the world's production, 'bound together with harmonised trade rules, harmonised investment rules, harmonised standards and certification, and an agreed way of settling disputes between members'. Diplomatic and trade initiatives have helped raise Australia's profile in Asia. An early 1989 Australian concept has grown into APEC (the Asia Pacific Economic Cooperation), a fifteen-member organisation dedicated to liberalising trade and investment in the region.

With the progress of economic integration in Europe and America's new commitment to the North American Free Trade Area (NAFTA), Australia is trying to assume the commercial mask of an Asian nation. All the present emphasis is on free trade and so-called multiculturalism. Young Australians, and New Zealanders too, are taking up Japanese and other Asian languages with a vengeance. In schools in the state of Victoria, four of the eight priority languages taught in primary school are Asian – Japanese, Mandarin, Indonesian and Vietnamese. A new Asia Education Foundation has embarked on a three-year, $2.4 million effort to introduce Asian themes throughout the entire Australian curriculum. Asian immigrants and the experiences of Australian businesses in Asia are even succeeding in changing the Australian work ethic. Today's longer opening hours are largely due to a need to keep up with the competition from smaller, Asian-run businesses.

In June 1990, former Australian Prime Minister Bob Hawke angered the government of China by creating a special immigration category to cater for Chinese students. This allowed 20,000 of their number who were in Australia at the time of the Tiananmen massacre to stay. At the same time, though, he was forcing Cambodian boat people, whom he accused of economic refugeeism, to return home. Hawke clearly understood the very positive effect that allowing large numbers of Chinese immigrants into the country could have on the economy. However, even Australian-Chinese were critical. Wellington Lee, chairman of the Asian-Australian Consultative Council and of the Chinese Chamber of Commerce, declared at the time that few of the Chinese students in Australia were genuine refugees; most were 'living off the blood' of Tiananmen Square.

Today the Australian government expects Asian-Australians to make up 25% of the population within fifty years, compared with the 4% they constitute today. The first Asian immigrants to Australia are said to have arrived as long ago as the Pleistocene epoch. Greater numbers followed much later when the British fleet stopped at Shanghai with its cargo of convicts to load up on supplies. As in the United States, however, the floodgates opened with the gold rush, when tens of thousands of Chinese headed for Australia. By 1860, Victoria had a Chinese population of well over 30,000. For the first seventy years of this century, Asian immigration was controlled by the country's 'Whites Only' policy. Fifty years ago, a full three-quarters of all first-generation Australians were born in the United Kingdom or the Republic of Ireland. By 1989, that figure had fallen to one-third. While Britain remains for the moment the leading source of Australian incomers, eight of the top ten sources of immigrants in 1991–2 were Asian countries.

Australia is learning its Chinese lessons in guanxi very well. Just one of the many current success stories is that of BHP, the metals and minerals giant, who won the right to operate Vietnam's only offshore oil-production platform. This was no doubt in large part due to Australia's diplomatic clout in Indochina. Another triumph is that of Australian Telecom, which is working with the electronics firm AWA to install a new telephone system in Vietnam. AWA is a major success itself, with a quarter of its $172 million in sales revenue likely to come from exports, half of them to Asia. Other Australian projects in Asia include new road systems for Hong Kong and four cities in China, a racecourse for Malaysia, and a recent $18.5 million contract to put new navigation systems in fifty-three of China's airports. By awarding contracts to Australian firms in their territories, the stage is set for the new taipans to make reciprocal forays into Australia in areas other than pure property development.

It would be impossible to document all the global activities that the new taipans are currently involved in. These are increasing all the time, with a renewed assertiveness that has only recently become apparent. Some ventures are particularly interesting in that the taipans behind them would not, until recently, have been thought of as being aggressive in anything other than their own domestic markets. Among the more visible and self-confident players are Kuok's Shangri-La group; Lo's Regal Hotels International; Cheung Yu-Tung's New World Developments; Li Ka-Shing's Cheung Kong Holdings; Gordon Wu's Hopewell; Lee Shau-Kee; and C. P. Pokhphand. Others are discussed below.

Media magnate Sir Run Run Shaw owns 34% of the Hong Kong-based company TVB (Television Broadcasts) Ltd, of which Robert Kuok's Kerry Group owns a further 28%. The company already had significant operations in China when it launched The Jade Channel in San Francisco in 1991, and in 1992 joined with the Vancouver-based Fairchild Group to start on an acquisition programme of TV stations in Canada. It has also recently signed an agreement allowing the Chinese Channel (a joint venture between the London-listed Wilton group and a private local company, Shaw Media Corporation) to provide Chinese language programming in Europe through satellite television. TVB has also leased four transponders on the Apstar 2 satellite.

Sally Aw Sian, chairman of Sing Tao Holdings, is Asia's answer to Lord Beaverbrook. On any given day, she can be found anywhere in the Pacific Rim, from Hong Kong to Australia, from Singapore to the US. Sing Tao, one of Hong Kong's oldest newspaper publishers, has a truly global network, with publishing and printing facilities around the world servicing virtually every major city where there is a Chinese community.

Singapore's Kwek Leng Beng is new taipan of the Hong Leong group. Its numerous activities include finance and property development; it is a major shareholder in CDL Hotels in Hong Kong and New Zealand; and through various subsidiaries it also owns the Manila Plaza Hotel and Taipei's Grand Hyatt Hotel. The group's international property holdings also include The Gloucester and The Chelsea hotels in London, The Regent/Four Seasons Hotel in Kuala Lumpur and the Millennium and Plaza hotels in New York.

The Kwek family also bought the Dao Heng Bank group from Grindlays Bank and renamed it the Guoco group. It is listed in Hong Kong, and also has branches in China, Macau, the UK, Sri Lanka and the Cayman Islands. These include the twenty-four branches of the Hang Lung Bank, which was bought from the Hong Kong government in 1989 for HK$600 million. Guoco have a UK subsidiary, Dao Heng Bank (London) PLC, which was formerly known as the Benchmark Bank PLC and was bought for HK$118 million. The group also owns 100% of the Overseas Trust Bank Ltd, which has subsidiary interests in various finance and card companies, as well as property, investment and travel. In 1993, Guoco also became involved in joint ventures in China for the manufacture of air conditioners, ceramic tiles and telecommunication cables.

Victor C. W. Lo's Gold Peak Industries (Holdings) Ltd is just one of many Hong Kong-based groups with multinational ambitions. The company specialises in the development, manufacture and marketing of batteries, electrical installation products, car audio equipment, speakers, and electronic parts and components, and to date has manufacturing and joint venture operations in China, Taiwan, Singapore, Malaysia, South Korea, Australia, Indonesia, Thailand, Sri Lanka, Canada, Denmark, France, Germany, Poland, Italy, the US and the UK. Gold Peak seems unstoppable.

Other major overseas players include the Chan brothers, Ronnie and Bernard, whose fortune is based on the soy sauce empire Amoy Canning (HK) Ltd, a company that was incorporated in 1949. They have a substantial portfolio of properties not only in Hong Kong through Amoy Properties and Hang Lung but also all over North America. They also hold a majority stake in a $500 million joint venture property development in Shanghai.

The Bank of East Asia, run by Cambridge-educated David Li Fook-Wo, now has sixteen branches overseas and sixty-seven local branches. For the last six years, it has been heavily involved, together with China Resources, Siam Ltd, and Sime Darby Ltd, in developing and promoting trade between China, Hong Kong, Thailand and Malaysia. A joint venture with the Aetna Insurance Company has led to the formation of the East Asia Aetna Insurance Company (Bermuda) Ltd, which provides a full range of life insurance services.

The Dharmala group of Jakarta-based taipan Suhargo Gondokusumo was originally a trading company specialising in primary commodities. It is now the sixth largest conglomerate in Indonesia and is involved in trading, manufacturing, plantations, property, financial services and construction all over the world. It has a strong presence in Australia and the United States, as well as four offices in Europe and operations in China, the Philippines, Hong Kong and Taiwan. Day-to-day business is said to be run by Suhargo's son Suyanto, an MBA graduate from the University of Southern California, who has worked for the company for more than a decade. Suhargo himself was born Go Ha Kim in Fujian province, but emigrated to Indonesia in 1941.

Another taipan with a strong Australian connection is James Riady, son of Dr Mochtar Riady, the founder and chairman of the powerful Lippo group. James studied accounting and economics in that country before holding various positions in the group, which has a major industrial subsidiary as well as significant interests in banking, property, life insurance, finance and information technology.

Liem Sioe Liong's Salim group, which currently accounts for about 5% of Indonesia's GDP, is the largest and most diverse Indonesian conglomerate. It is now working hard on becoming a world player, and to this end is represented internationally by two main holding companies, KMP Ltd and the First Pacific group. Interests include flour-milling, cars, steel, banking, food-processing and chemicals. Tourism is a further concern, and the group has been working on developing a massive tourist complex on Bintan Island near Singapore. Daily operations are run by Anthony Salim, Liong's son, who will eventually move into his father's shoes. The company has close connections with Indonesia's President Suharto and his family.

Andres Soriano III, an economics graduate from the Wharton School of Finance, is a major Filipino taipan. Together with his

73

brothers, Eduardo and Carlos, he runs the family flagship company, San Miguel Corporation, one of the biggest publicly held Philippines businesses. Its roots date back more than a hundred years, and it has the largest employee base in the private sector, with more than 36,000 workers. The company dominates the soft drinks industry across the country and is currently linked with Coca Cola (USA). It is also involved in significant enterprise elsewhere in the world, including Switzerland (with Nestlé), Spain, Taiwan, China and Nepal. Andres Soriano III is also linked with Thornton Management (Asia) Ltd and with (HK) Tyndall International (Asia), and he jointly manages the Philippine Long-Term Equity Fund and the First Philippine Investment Trust.

It is clear from these brief portraits that the new taipans are out on the world stage, and that they intend to stay there. Each move has been considered and executed with consummate precision. The strands of local and taipan-to-taipan involvement are so densely interwoven that there will be no unravelling. In each case, the taipans are meeting their own number-one criterion: to become indispensable in any community where they find themselves, whether it be at home or abroad. There will be no turning back.

Chapter 7

Who's Who Among the New Taipans

HONG KONG

Ann, T. K. is chairman of Winsor Industrial, with food and textile manufacturing interests as well as property investment (the Winner and Lucky Buildings and 75% of the Regent Centre). The company has just embarked on a 40% joint venture in manufacturing in Burma.

Au, Alexander is CEO of Hang Seng Bank (see Sir Lee Quo-Wei).

Aw Sian, Sally is chairman of Sing Tao Holdings, in which she retains a 70.8% stake. The company has worldwide involvements in newspaper publishing (*Sing Tao* and *The Hong Kong Standard*), printing, property and retailing. It was the first foreign company to enter China's newspaper market, by printing a TV guide for Guangzhou province.

Chan, Raymond (Fat-chu) is chairman of Tem Fat Hing Fung Holdings Ltd, which started out in 1949 as a gold bullion trader and has moved on into other jewellery and metals, as well as property and financial services. The company is involved in the refinement and production of gold and other precious metals in Malaysia, and in trading in Hong Kong, China and elsewhere in Asia. More recently it has undertaken property development in Shanghai.

Chan, Ronnie, together with the Chen family, owns 37.63% of Hang Lung Development Co., and its property arm Amoy Properties Ltd, with property in Hong Kong (Grand Hotel, Tsim Sha Tsui, Laguna City Commercial Complex in Kwun Tong and Standard Chartered

Bank Building in Central) and China (Shanghai), as well as interests in car parks, dry cleaning, department stores and restaurants. In 1980, Chan acquired a controlling interest in the Amoy Canning Corporation (HK) Ltd, which started out nearly fifty years ago producing soy sauce and canning fruits and vegetables.

Chang, Chu-Cheng is chairman of Varitronix, a major manufacturer of LCDs in Hong Kong, China and Malaysia. The company has sales offices in the United Kingdom and in France.

Chang, Stephen (Lien-Hing) is chairman of Innovative International Holdings, which is involved in telecommunications and car accessories manufacturing (the Rhino Group). He also deals in property in China.

Chao, Kuang-Piu, together with his family, owns 59.2% of Novel Enterprises, which is involved in the manufacture of knitwear and other clothing, in property, and in marketing through the Pepe Group (UK) and the US-based Tommy Hilfiger retail operation. They are the owners of the 'Noveli' brand of jeans.

Chearavanont, Dhanin (see also under Thailand). His C.P. Pokhphand group, which is involved in agribusiness, industrial manufacturing and trading, also owns 55.8% of Orient Telecom & Technology Holdings Ltd, with property investments, power generation, infrastructural (Don Muang Tollway project linking Bangkok to the international airport) and telecommunications projects. OT&T was bought from the Yue Hwa department store in 1989. The group also owns several Kentucky Fried Chicken outlets.

Cheng, Yu-Tung is chairman of the New World Development Co. Ltd, owners since 1989 of the United States-based hotel chain, Ramada. His company is a property investment concern that is also engaged in the development of infrastructural projects, telecommunications, insurance, and The Dynasty Club. It also owns 27% of Asia Television Ltd.

Chow, Raymond is chairman of the Manhattan Card Co. Ltd, which once constituted Chase Manhattan Bank's card operations but since

1993 has been incorporated in Hong Kong in its own right. The company is 20% owned by CITIC Pacific Ltd (see Yung, Larry).

Chua, Robert, 'Mr Television' in Hong Kong. He comes originally from Singapore and together with his wife Peggy has made the greatest inroads of any foreigner into lucrative tv franchises in mainland China.

Fu, Adrian is chairman of Furama Hotel Enterprises, which started commercial life in 1958 and which owns the Majestic Centre and Hotel, the Furama Kempinski Hotel and Majestic International Hotels.

Ho, George is chairman of ABC Communications, which he set up in 1971 to provide radio-paging services in Hong Kong. Ten years ago, Ho launched the world's first continuously updated financial data service, using alpha-numeric pagers in conjunction with Reuters. The company is 63% owned by HCBC Enterprises Ltd and is active now in Taiwan, the Philippines, Guangdong, Vietnam and Shanghai.

Ho, Stanley is chairman of Shun Tak Holdings, which is involved in transport (the Hong Kong–Macau jetfoils, 20% of Air Hong Kong), property (Nova Taipa, Macau, and 60% of the Guangzhou Cultural Centre), hotels (Westin Resort and Macau Golf and Country Club, the Macau Casino monopoly, a share in the Macau Jockey Club, and 50% of the Mandarin Oriental Macau) and in retailing and restaurants.

Kadoorie, Michael is a member of the Kadoorie family who own Hongkong & Shanghai Hotels. This company in turn owns the Peninsula Group, and a number of commercial and residential complexes. The Kadoories also own 34% of China Light & Power, the electricity company which supplies Guangdong and Kowloon and which is responsible for the Black Point and Daya Bay nuclear power stations. The 'old taipan', the late Lord Lawrence Kadoorie, retired in 1992 and was succeeded as chairman by Sir Sidney Gordon. Together with Cheung Kong (see Li, Ka-Shing), the company developed the Hok Un power station into a residential estate.

77

Kan, Paul (Man-Lok) is chairman of Champion Technology Holdings, which was started in 1987 when Kan left Cable & Wireless to develop a Chinese-language paging service. It now operates multilingual paging systems in China and Taiwan and has entered into a joint venture for a paging system in the Russian Federation. Kan also now owns Multitone UK, which manufactures pagers, paging equipment and fax machines.

Keswick, Henry is the definitive 'old taipan' as chairman of Jardine Matheson Holdings. The company's primary listing is in London, but it is also listed in Australia, Singapore, the United States and Luxembourg. It is no longer listed in Hong Kong. Major interests include Dairy Farm, Hongkong Land and 51% of the Mandarin Oriental Hotel Group, as well as Jardine Fleming, Jardine Insurance, and Jardine Strategic Holdings. The latter owns 25.3% of the UK's Trafalgar House, through Hongkong Land.

Kuok, Robert (Hock-Nien) is the taipan of his own group of companies, which owns 59% of the Shangri-la Asia Hotel group. The group's interests have extended beyond Malaysia to Hong Kong, China and elsewhere in the region. Kuok is also chairman of SCMP Holdings, owner of *The South China Morning Post* newspaper and its attendant magazine publishing and bookshop operations.

Kwek, Leng-Beng (see also under Singapore) is chairman of CDL Hotels International, owner of numerous hotels including Taipei's Grand Hyatt, Singapore's Novotel Orchid, London's Chelsea Hotel, and New Zealand's Quality Hotels.

Kwok, Karl (Chi-Leung), one of the Wing On Kwoks, originally from Shanghai. The family own their eponymous department stores, the Hotel Fortuna, and life assurance and trading company interests.

Kwok, Walter (Ping-Sheung), chairman of Sun Hung Kai properties, which is 43.5% owned by the Kwok family and was originally listed in 1972. Apart from property, the company is heavily involved, through associated businesses, in telecommunications (SmartTone and SmartCom), cinemas, garment manufacturing and hotels (the Royal Garden Hotel, Tsimshatsui; and the Royal Park Hotel, Shatin).

Lai, Jimmy (Chee-Ying) is chairman of Giordano Holdings, in which he has a 36.3% stake. The company is involved in the retail and distribution of clothing and accessories, under its own brand name, and has various regional interests in Japan, Singapore, Taiwan, Macau and Malaysia. He also has publishing interests.

Lee, Hon-Chiu is chairman of the Hysan Development Company, which has projects in Beijing, Shanghai, and Hong Kong. It has acquired Hong Kong's Lee Gardens Hotel for redevelopment into a commercial building.

Lee, Marcus (Tse Bun) is chairman of his family-owned (62.5%) Le Saunda Holdings, which is involved in the retail of Italian shoes. The company has shops throughout Hong Kong and in China, Macau and Singapore.

Sir Lee Quo-Wei is chairman of the Hang Seng Bank, which is 61.5% owned by the Hongkong and Shanghai Bank. The bank is the world's fifth richest in terms of assets, and has overseas offices in New York, San Francisco, Shanghai, Shenzhen and Xiamen, as well as more than 130 domestic branches.

Lee, Shau-Kee owns 67.8% of Henderson Land Development, which in turn owns the Newton Hotels in Hong Kong and Kowloon; department stores in Tsuen Wan and Tsuen Mun in the New Territories; developments in Beijing, Guangzhou, Shanghai and Shenzhen; and also chunks of Henderson Investment and of Hong Kong & China Gas, of which Lee is also chairman. The Lee family also own a 34.78% interest in Miramar Hotel and Investment Co.

Lee, Wing Sum is chairman of Wo Kee Hong (Holdings) Ltd, in which he holds a 56.5% stake. The companies in the holding group are engaged in the manufacture of air conditioners, the distribution of Pioneer and Sansui electronics, and audio-visual equipment. Together with Japan's Pioneer Electronics, they established Pioneer Electronics China Ltd in Shanghai, and they also have a 50% interest in a joint venture for Rogers speakers.

Leung, Ray-Man is CEO of S. Megga International Holdings Ltd, in which he holds a 24.6% stake. The company manufactures telecommunications products for companies like AT&T. It is active in a number of joint ventures in China and has been expanding into property development, investing and trading.

Li, David (Li Fook-Wo) is a member of the Li, Fung and Kan grouping of families. Cambridge-educated Li runs the Bank of East Asia, which has recently developed a close relationship with the mainland Chinese banking and investment authorities, and has joint ventures with the Bank of China and China Resources (HK) Ltd.

Li, Gonzaga is chairman of The Wharf Holdings Ltd (formerly known as The Hong Kong and Kowloon Wharf and Godown Company Ltd), one of the biggest owners and developers of property in Hong Kong. The company has stakes in the Marco Polo Hotel in Singapore, Harbour City's Gateway Towers, the Kwai Chung container terminal, and the Western Harbour Crossing project. It also owns a 75% interest in Rediffusion.

Li, Ka-Shing, the taipans' taipan, has as 34.9% stake in Cheung Kong, the holding company which owns Hutchison Whampoa (Hutchison Telecom, Park 'N' Shop, A.S. Watson, Fortress), Cavendish and Hong Kong Electric Holdings. The company is one of the largest property developers and investors in Hong Kong. George Magnus succeeded Simon Murray in 1993 as chairman of Hong Kong Electric.

Lim, Por Yen is chairman of Lai Sun Garment (Intl) Ltd, which is involved in hotels, restaurants and property, and in the manufacture of garments for its 'Crocodile' label, which it acquired a few years ago.

Lo, Fong-Seong is chairman of Fairwood Holdings, which is mostly owned by Dennis and Alfred Lo, who operate the Mario Italian restaurant chain and the Thousand Island food plazas. They are currently expanding into China, Macau and Singapore.

Lo, Kat-Muk is chairman of Café de Coral, a chain of fast-food outlets which is 47% owned by the Lo family. They also own fifteen branches of The Spaghetti House, three of Diners Court and four Very Nice Fast Food outlets. They are currently expanding into China.

Lo, Victor is the chairman of Gold Peak Industries (Holdings) Ltd, which manufactures batteries, electrical products, and car and audio equipment in Hong Kong, China, Malaysia, Singapore, Taiwan, Thailand, South Korea, Australia, Canada and Europe.

Lo, Y. S. (Ying Shek) is chairman of Great Eagle Holdings Ltd, which began in 1963 as a property developer and now owns Hong Kong's 'most intelligent building', Citibank Plaza. It also owns the Hong Kong Renaissance Hotel, the Astor Theatre, and The London Theatre entertainment complex.

Lo, Y. S. (Yuk Sui) is chairman of Paliburg International, a holding company involved in property, construction, and project management. He is also chairman of Regal Hotels International (Regal Hong Kong, Regal Airport, Regal Riverfront, Regal Shanghai, etc.).

Luk, King-Tin is chairman of Luks Industrial, in which his family have a 37% stake. Incorporated in 1975, the company has operations in China and Vietnam in plywood, cement, property, television and electronics. For the last few years, it has been expanding into Eastern Europe and the former Soviet Union.

Ma, Ching-Kwan is chairman of Oriental Press, which was set up over twenty-five years ago to publish the *Oriental Daily*, Hong Kong's most widely read newspaper. The group recently launched a new English-language newspaper, *Eastern Express*.

Ma, Joyce. A member of the (originally) Shanghainese Kwok family of the Wing On department store group, Joyce Ma introduced Hong Kong to the likes of Gianni Versace and Giorgio Armani when they were still comparatively unknown even in the US. Today she holds a number of very lucrative fashion franchises for Hong Kong and elsewhere in the Asian Continent.

Ng, Robert (Chee-Siong) is chairman of Sino Land (The Royal Cliff, Omega Plaza, Pacific Plaza, Hacienda, Central Plaza, etc.), which is 62% owned by the Ng family vehicle, Tsimshatsui Properties.

Poon, Dickson is chairman of Dickson Concepts, owner of a number of regional and worldwide distributorships for luxury goods. Dickson Concepts owns and manages retail outlets in Hong Kong, Taiwan, Thailand, Singapore and China – and in London, Harvey Nichols department store.

Poon, Hon Kam is chairman of High Fashion International Ltd, manufacturers for Benetton, Laura Ashley, Liz Claiborne and a number of its own labels.

Purves, William is an 'old taipan' in that he is the current chairman of the Hongkong and Shanghai Banking Group, which was founded in Hong Kong in 1865 and owns the Midland Bank PLC. The HSBC Group is one of the largest in the world, with major commercial and investment banking businesses all round the globe.

Quek Leng Chan (see also under Malaysia) is the chairman of Dao Heng Bank group, the holding company for the Dao Heng Bank and the Overseas Trust Bank, with eighty-nine branches in Hong Kong and eight overseas. He is also chairman of the Guoco group, which has several joint ventures in China.

Salim, Soedono (see also under Indonesia). Headquartered in Hong Kong, his First Pacific Company is a conglomerate involved in property, telecommunications and banking, with operations and interests in twenty-five different countries and with more than 18,000 employees worldwide.

Shaw, Sir Run Run is the chairman of Shaw Brothers Hong Kong, in which he retains a 70% stake. He set the company up in 1958 to become the leading producer and distributor of movies in the Asian-Pacific region. He holds a minority stake in TVB Broadcasting, a Hong Kong television station of which he was a founding member.

Sutch, Peter is chairman of Swire Pacific, one of Hong Kong's leading publicly quoted companies, with interests in aviation (Cathay Pacific and air terminals), property (Swire Properties), industries (Taiwan Coca-Cola Bottling), trading (Reebok HK), marine services and insurance. He is also chairman of Hong Kong Aircraft Engineering Company (HAECO), created out of Jardine Matheson's and Butterfield & Swire's air maintenance divisions and originally incorporated in 1950.

Ting, James bought the Singer Sewing Machine Company in 1989. He holds a Canadian PhD and is the brains behind the phenomenally successful Semi-Tech Global electronics company.

Tsang, Wing Hong is chairman of the Wing Hang Bank, which was started in 1947 by Y. K. Fung and is associated with the Bank of New York through the latter's 35.1% share ownership in Wing Hang. The Fung family still retains 19.75% of the stock.

Wang, Patrick is the MD of Johnson Electric, founded in 1959 by his parents Mr and Mrs Seng Liang to manufacture micromotors for toys and household appliances. Under Wang, who is a masters graduate from Purdue University, the company has set up R & D bases in both Germany and Switzerland, as well as operations in Thailand, China and Japan. The Chinese translation of Johnson, 'Zhou Chun', means 'making things inch by inch'.

Whang, Tar Choung is chairman of both Lam Soon (HK) Ltd and of Lam Soon Food Industries, a thirty-five-year-old operation with interests in food-processing, detergents, and the trading of electronic and packaging products. He is also chairman of MC Packaging (HK) Ltd, engaged in the manufacture of plastic and metal containers.

Wong, David (Shou-Yeh) is chairman of Dah Sing Financial Holdings, the ninth largest local banking group in Hong Kong in terms of assets, and tenth in terms of profits. Founded in 1947, the bank now has branches in Los Angeles, San Francisco and Shenzhen, as well as fifty branches in Hong Kong. The Wong family still own 40% of the shares. Since 1991, Ronald Carstairs, previously of Standard Chartered Bank, has been managing director.

Woo, Peter is one of the late Sir Y. K. Pao's sons-in-law. Mr and Mrs Peter Woo own the majority interest in Wheelock and Company Limited (previously known as World International Holdings), which was incorporated in Shanghai in 1918. Wheelock is involved in property and infrastructure development, retailing (Lane Crawford Intl) and trade, and hotels and communications. Wheelock Pacific has joint ventures with Virgin Megastores in Hong Kong, and with Foster's, the Australian brewery company.

Wu, Gordon (Ying-Sheung) is chairman of Hopewell Holdings, developers of major infrastructural projects including the Guangzhou-Shenzhen-Zhuhai Superhighway, and of the Mega Tower Hotel complex next to the Hopewell Centre. Together with Cheung Kong Holdings, Hopewell also developed the HITEC exhibition centre complex in Kowloon Bay. Wu is also involved in Consolidated Electric Power Asia (CEPA), which has power plant operations in both mainland China and the Philippines and has plans to expand to Indonesia, Taiwan and Vietnam.

Wu, Jianchang is Deng Xiao Ping's eldest son-in-law (husband of Deng Lin). He controls CNNC (the China National Non-ferrous Metals Industry Corp.) which is also engaged in property and investment ventures.

Wu, Michael (Po-Ko) is chairman and CEO of the Wing Lung Bank, which has a branch in Los Angeles and twenty-eight branches in Hong Kong. The Wu family, who established the bank in 1933, still retain some 52% of the stock, having sold 10% to the Development Bank of Singapore in 1992.

Yu, Pun-Hoi is the somewhat controversial former chairman of Ming Pao Enterprises Corporation Ltd. He has fallen foul of the Securities and Exchange Commission in Hong Kong by failing to disclose a four-month Canadian jail sentence for credit and card fraud. Ming Pao, a leading publisher, is also involved in other media, and in tourism (Charming Holidays). It has published a North American edition of the newspaper *Ming Pao* for nearly twenty years, and has also launched both Toronto and Vancouver editions.

Yung, Larry is chairman of CITIC Pacific, which is 44% owned by CITIC HK. CITIC was set up in 1980 as the first major mainland presence in Hong Kong, and is involved in a number of companies, including Cathay Pacific (12.5%), Dragonair (46.1%), Hong Kong Telecom, and Macau Telecom, as well as waste treatment and Chinese infrastructural developments.

Zie Yongder, Alan — an enigma and a talented artist and sculptor, Zie owns a number of franchises for well known magazines including the Chinese edition of *Cosmopolitan*.

INDONESIA

Bakrie, Aburizal and *Bakrie, Nirwan D.* run the Bakrie Brothers group, which was set up by their father Achmad and his brother Aboejamin in the 1950s. The company started out in coffee beans, rubber and pepper, and expanded into steel pipe making, palm oil and other crops.

Darmawan, Hari is Indonesia's retail king. He owns nearly 50 Matahari department stores throughout the country, and also owns supermarkets and bookstores.

Gondokusumo, Suhargo, together with his sons, Suyanto, Slamet, Santoso and Hendro Santoso, control and run the Dharmala group, which was established in the 1950s in the agriculture and animal feed business. They have since expanded into plastics, property, banking, insurance and housing development.

Mooryati, Sudibyo of Mustika Rato is the grand-daughter of a sultan. She began her herbal cosmetics business nearly 25 years ago and now has annual sales of around $40m.

Nursalim, Sjamsul runs the Gajah Tunggal group, a forty-year-old concern with its origins in the manufacture of tyres. Since then it has expanded into electrical and telecommunication cable manufacturing, the paint industry, and banking and the retail sector.

Pangestu, Prajogo founded the Barito timber-based conglomerate in the 1970s. Amongst his other assets are one-third of Andromeda Bank and an interest in PT Astra International.

Rachman, Halim, aka Tjoa To Hing, is the son of a Fujian immigrant to Indonesia. He owns the country's largest clove cigarette manufacturer, Gudang Garam.

Riady, Mochtar, a very prominent Indonesian banker, is the scion of the Lippo group family, which includes his sons, James, Andrew and Stephen. The group is mainly involved in the manufacture of electrical appliances, automotive distribution, banking, insurance, leasing, stockbroking and property.

Salim, Soedono (Liem Sioe Liong) started his eponymous conglomerate over forty years ago. It is now the largest group in Indonesia, and also has business activities throughout South-East and East Asia, the US, Western Europe, Australia and New Zealand. It is involved these days in everything from the financial sector and property to cars, chemicals, cement, oil-refining and flour-milling.

Sentosa, Ferry Teguh founded the Ometraco group over thirty years ago with the distribution and sole representation in Indonesia of a number of imported manufactured goods. Today the group is also involved in agribusiness, finance, property and chicken breeding.

Wanandi, Sofjan, is chairman of the Gemala Group of auto component and pharmaceutical companies. The group owns among others the Chicago company Trailmobile and a number of battery manufacturers in the UK and Australia.

Widjaja, Eka Tijpta founded the Sinar Mas group in the early sixties. It is now the largest producer of edible oils in the country. It is also heavily involved in pulp and paper manufacturing, and has been expanding into banking, leasing, insurance, and property management and development.

KOREA (SOUTH)

Baik, Sung-Hak, the Manchurian-born hat king, is worth around $300 million and produces some 60 million hats a year, mostly baseball caps under licence from the major US leagues. He has manufacturing operations throughout N. America, Bangladesh, Sri Lanka and mainland China.

Cho, Jung-Hoon is the taipan of the Korean Air-focused Hanjin group. Starting out in transport for American GIs during the Korean War, the business has expanded into construction, securities and other transport-related subsidiaries.

Choi, Chong-Hyun is the younger brother of the founder of the Sungkyong group, Choi Chong-Kon. Today the group concentrates mostly on textiles, chemicals, telecommunications and general trading. The present taipan's son, Choi Tae-Won, is married to the daughter of Korea's former president Roh Tae-Woo.

Choi, Wonsuk is the brains behind the Dong Ah group and the son of the group's founder, Choi Jun-Mun. Dong Ah is a major force in construction overseas, and is involved through Korea Express in trucking, and through Dong Ah Securities in securities.

Choong, Kim Woo is the workaholic and perfectionist chairman of Daewoo, one of Korea's leading and most powerful chaebols.

Chung, Ju-Young is the founder of the Hyundai group, which owns some of the largest car, ship, steel, cement and paint companies in the world. The nominal group chairman is the founder's younger brother, Chung Sei-Young, who is president of Hyundai Motors.

Chung, Sang-Young founded and still runs the Keumkang group, which is mainly focused on building materials and chemicals. The group has close links with Hyundai. Chung's brother, Chung In-Young, runs the Halla group, based in the cement and auto parts manufacturing sectors.

Kim, Seung-Yon is the son of Kim Jong-Hee, founder of the Hanwha group.

Kim, Suk-Won is the son of Kim Sung-Kon, the founder of the Ssangyong group. The group's main interests lie in ordnance supplies, oil refining, and the manufacture of machinery and chemicals.

Ku, Ja-Kyong is the eldest son of the late Ku In-Hoi, the founder of the Lucky-Goldstar group. The group's widely diversified business interests are based mostly on chemicals, construction and electronics.

Shin Kyuk-ho is Korea's candy king. He spent his youth in Japan earning pocket money from a paper round: today his Lotte Group is worth around $6 billion.

Lee, Hwakyung is a son-in-law of Lee Yang-Ku, the founder of the Tongyang group. Subsidiary companies in the group are involved in cement, confectionery, securities and investment, and in the

DACOM Corporation, the international telecommunications company.

Lee, Kun-Hee, third son of Lee Byong-Chull, the founder of the Samsung group, heads up the company, with its interests in chemicals, electronics, paper, textiles and heavy industry. The group is Korea's largest and most profitable conglomerate.

MALAYSIA

Tan Sri Radin Soenarno Al-Haj is chairman of United Engineers Malaysia.

Abdul Rashid bin Hussein is one of Malaysia's foremost stockbrokers.

Tengku Dato' Adnan Bin Tengku Mansor operates the Berjaya Sports Toto and Berjaya Leisure & Lottery, and is engaged in setting up lotteries in Shenyang, Chengdu and Dalian in China.

Dato' Haji Ahmad Asisuddin Bin Haji Zainal Abidin controls IJM Inc., whose business interests lie in construction and property development. The company is active in the US, Britain, Australia, Hong Kong, Singapore and Pakistan.

Tan Sri Dato' Seri Tunku Ahmad Bin Tunku Yahaya runs the plantation arm of Sime Darby.

Ananda Krishnan, a Sri Lankan Tamil based in Kuala Lumpur, began by trading petroleum and then established the powerful Tanjong gaming empire, and is a property developer. He also owns telecommunications companies. He is involved in building Malaysia's tallest buildings, Petronas Towers in KL.

Ang Guan Seng is MD of Petaling Garden, a property and housing developer which has for the last twelve years been involved in hotel ownership. The company is working on major developments within the Klang Valley, as well as having interests in insurance, plantations and golf course management. They have recently put together a 40-60 joint venture with Shangri-la Hotels for the Shangri-la Hotel, Penang.

Tan Sri Dato' Haji (Dr) Ani Bin Arope is chairman of Tenaga Nasional, formerly the nationalised electricity supplier, which has now been privatised.

Tan Sri Dato' Azman Hashim owns 60% of AM Corp (Arab-Malaysian Corporation), (largely through the dealings of William Cheung) which is involved in property, investment, the manufacture of children's clothing, the Kuala Lumpur Monorail, waste treatment and construction. His other activities include a finance company, AMSG Stockbroking, credit leasing, merchant banking and insurance. He is also chairman of AMMB Holdings, a merchant banking service.

Tan Sri Wan Azmi Wan Hamzah is a 'student' of former finance minister Daim Zainuddin and, like him, an investor *extraordinaire*. He is also the treasurer of UMND and chairman of R. J. Reynolds (Malaysia), of which he also owns 20.7%. He is chairman too of Land & General, which owns the Australian-listed Odin Mining and Investment Company. He owns 25% of Rashid Hussain, the securities firm, and other business ventures include property development, the manufacture of plastic resins, furniture and logging.

Dato' Mohamed Basir Ahmad is chairman of Malayan Banking, Malaysia's largest banking group, which has branches in Singapore, Brunei, London, New York and Hong Kong.

Joseph Chong, taipan of Westmont Holdings, is a business associate of William Cheng of ASM, the largest steel mill in Malaysia.

Tan Sri Geh Ik Cheong is chairman of the Development & Commercial Bank, the fifth largest commercial bank in Malaysia, and of Perlis. He is one of Malaysia's 'great and good' rather than an entrepreneur.

Dato' Mohd Ghaus Bin Badioze Zamanch is the head of the Malaysian Tobacco Co.

General Tan Sri Dato' Mohd Ghazali Haji Che Mat is chairman of Boustead Holdings, which was formed in 1963 out of the UK's Turner & Newall, the manufacturers of asbestos cement pipes.

Dato' Halim Bin Saad owns 38% of Renong, with interests in manu-facturing, steel mills, bus services, investment, hotels, and property, as well as in the Faber Group, Time Engineering, and Commerce Asset Holding Financial Services. He is also involved in oil and gas, cement, construction, project management, and the North–South highway concession company.

Dato' H'ng Bok San and family own 40% of Universal Holdings, manufacturers of telecom cables, power cables and wire, the largest company of its kind in Malaysia. They are involved in a joint venture with Goldstar to manufacture cable in Shantou, China.

Hong Lee-Pee is chairman of Pilecon Engineering, a construction company with projects in Malaysia, Singapore, Brunei, Hong Kong and Thailand. They are currently engaged in a joint venture with the Johore government for Johore coastal development.

Tunku Imran Ibni Tuanku Ta'afar (known as 'Tunku Pete'). His father is the present king, the Sultan of Negri Sembilau ('Tunku Bill') is in charge at the Aluminium Company of Malaysia (ALCAN and ALCOM).

Tun Ismail Bin Mohamed Ali is a former governor of the Central Bank, Chairman of PNB (and hence of many other companies) and the brother-in-law of the Prime Minister. He is famously austere, incorruptible and terrifying. He is also chairman of Sime Darby and the Pataling Rubber Estates Ltd, Golden Hope Plantations Ltd, and The London Asiatic Rubber and Produce Company Ltd. He is also chairman of a new creation of ex-Guthrie interests called Amanah Saham Bumiputera, Permodalan Nasional, Amanah Saham Nasional.

Tunku Naquiyuddin Ibni Tuanku Ta'afar controls Kian Joo Kan Fac-tory & Tractors Malaysia Holdings, who are the sole distributors of Caterpillar heavy equipment and Ford agricultural and industrial machinery in Malaysia.

Jaffar bin Hussein is governor of Bank Negara, Malaysia's central bank, which these days is purportedly independent of the Ministry of Finance.

Tan Sri Dato' Jamil Bin Mohamed Jan manages Kedah Cement Holdings, and EON, the distributor of Proton, the Malaysian national car. He is also involved in stockbroking, and companies for the rust-proofing of cars, and the chairman of the Proton manufacturing company, Perusahaan Otomobil Nasional.

Tan Sri Dato' Dr Shamsuddin Bin Abdul Kadir is chairman of Uniphone Telecommunications, formerly known as Malayan Cables and the Sapura Group.

Puan Sri Kharijah Ahmad. She is the chairwoman and founder of the KAF financial group of KAF Discount.

Tan Sri Dato Khoo Kay Peng is former chairman of Malayan United Industries, once only manufacturers of household utensils, toothbrushes and paper, but now involved in the hotel business and in cement. They own the Ming Court Hotel in Kuala Lumpur and Ming Court properties in Penang and Port Dickson.

Khoo Teik Choi is chairman of Tanjong PLC, originally a tin-mining company but now heavily into gambling, with the second largest share after the Magnum Corporation of a very healthy market. Tanjong is responsible for the new Kuala Lumpur racecourse.

The family of the late *Lee Loy Seng* own a large share of the KL (Kuala Lumpur) Kepong Group, one of the biggest oil, palm rubber and cocoa plantation operations in Malaysia. They are also active in finance, education and property management.

Datuk Lim Ah Tam and *Lim Bok Yen* run the Magnum Corporation, a numbers forecast operator, and four-digit gaming market leader. The company has several joint ventures in China, including a recreation club in Beijing, a hospital, a seven-storey commercial complex, and a residential development in Shenyang. Lim is also joint chairman of Bandear Raya Developments, the property arm of Multi Purpose Holdings, which currently has one of the largest land banks in Malaysia.

Tan Sri Lim Goh Tong and family own 49% of the world-renowned Genting International Ltd (investment holdings, including paper mills), 40% of Genting Berhad (Resorts World, gaming and hotels), and 58% of Asiatic Development (plantations).

Lim Thian-Kiat owns 9% of Kamuting Corp. Bhd, which is corporately related to Malaysian Plantation Bhd. He also owns 15% of the Magnum Corporation and 13% of Dunlop Estates Bhd, which provides Sarawak with electricity.

Tan Sri Loh Boon Siew is chairman of Oriental Holdings, the company that assembles Honda cars in both Singapore and Malaysia, and distributes John Deer, Hitachi and Krupp equipment.

Dr Loy Hean Heong is the controversial president and CEO of MBf Holdings with interests in finance, education and property management.

Tunku Tan Sri Mohamed Bin Tunku Besar Burhanuddin is chairman of Rothmans of Pall Mall (Malaysia), the first overseas listed arm of the UK parent company, Rothmans Intl.

Ghazali Mohamed Khalid is on the boards of Denko, Mah Sing, Golden Frontier and Super Enterprise. He is one of the most popular 'bumi' partners of choice for Chinese businessmen in Malaysia.

Dato' Seri Syed Nahar Tun Syed Sheik Shahbuddin is chairman of SIME UEP Properties, the property arm of the Sime Darby group. The company's developments are mostly in the Klang Valley.

Tunku Naquiyiddin is a royal prince of the Negri Sembilan family and a power behind Antah Holdings Bhd, a food and finance company which owns 32% of the UK Unigroup PLC.

Tan Sri Datuk Nasruddin Bin Mohamed is chairman of Sungei Way Holdings, which contains a number of companies with interests in quarrying, the manufacture of premix, building materials, and financial services. He is also the chairman of the Malaysian Mining Corporation, now engaged in the exploration and mining of diamonds, gold and other precious metals. This company owns 10% of the Australian-listed company, Plutonic Resources.

Tun Dato' Haji Omar Yoke Lin Ong is chairman of OYL Industries, manufacturer of air-conditioners and windows. He is also chairman of Malaysian Oxygen.

Tunku Osman Ahmad is chairman of Pelangi, the residential property development company, most of whose projects are centred in Johore. They also manufacture roof tiles and ready-mixed concrete, and are involved in rubber and oil palm plantations.

Dato' Mohd Desa Pachi is chairman of Commerce Asset-Holding, formerly a family-owned bank in Kuching, Sarawak.

The Quek family, with Quek, Leng Chan as chairman, own 46.7% of Hong Leong Co. (M) Bhd, as well as 44% of Hume Industries (building materials, air-conditioners, refrigerators, roofing tiles). They also own the Nanyang Press (media and papers), Ban Hin Lee Bank, HL Properties, Assurance and Leasing, Zalik Securities, and HL Industries (motorcycles, ceramic tiles, building materials, steel mills, corrugated paper cartons and semiconductors).

Abdullah Ibni Almarhum Tuanku Abdul Rahman is chairman of Associated International Cement (Blue Circle PLC), which owns 57.8% of Malayan Cement.

Rahmat Bin Jamari is chief executive of Kelang Container Terminal and the Malaysian International Shipping Corporation.

Tan Sri Dato' Dr Mohd Rashdan Bin Haji Baba is chairman of Telekom Malaysia, which was formerly a government department but has since been privatised. It is now the only integrated telecommunications company in Malaysia.

Tan Sri Sallehuddin Bin Mohamed is chairman of Cycle & Carriage Bintang (48.9% owned by C & C Ltd and 12.5% owned by Jardine Intl Motor Holding).

Teh Soen Seng was a prime mover behind the listing of the timber company Aokam Perdana in 1992, with Abdul Rashid bin Hussein.

Tunku Tan Sri Dato' Shahriman Bin Tunku Sulaiman is chairman of

Malaywata Steel, as well as of Pernas International Hotels & Properties, the owners of the Pernas Hotel Chain.

Dato' Shamsir Omar is chairman of Time Engineering, the telecommunications and engineering arm of Renong (see also Dato' Halim Bin Saad).

Tajuddin Ramli owns 25% of Technology Resources Industries (telecommunications) and Celcom (cellular phones), and 13% of MHS helicopter services. He also controls 32% of MAS and 40% of PNSL shipping.

Tan, Vincent Chee-Yioun Sri Dato' owns 52% of Berjaya Group Bhd, whose many interests include travel; Hyumal motor distribution for Hyundai; and Industri Otomotif Komersial, National Commercial Vehicle manufacturers. He is also engaged in stockbroking and insurance, and owns 20% of Star publications. He is busy with resort development abroad and with overseas casinos in Mauritius and the Seychelles. Other involvements include Berjaya Singer, Berjaya Sports Toto, Sports Toto Malaysia, and Berjaya Lottery Management HK Ltd, a mainland China gaming operation.

Dato' Tan Kim Hor, of the Tan family, owns 34.3% of Tan Chong Motor Holdings, the sole assembler and distributor in Malaysia of Nissan vehicles.

Datuk Tan Kim Yeow is chairman of IGB Corporation, which is 28% owned by the Tan family. IGB owns 48.6% of the Ipoh Garden in Australia and 20% of Negara Properties in Malaysia, and is one of the country's largest listed property companies, with activities in Malaysia, Australia and the USA. Its main Australian asset is the retail-based Queen Victoria Building.

Teh Hong Piow owns 40% of Public Bank, a commercial bank, and 56% of London & Pacific, a general insurance company. The latter business owns JCG (HK) Ltd, a finance company, and 57% of Public Finance, and has other activities in stockbroking, with branches in Vietnam, Cambodia and Sri Lanka. The chairman of both Public Bank and Public Finance is Tan Sri Dato' Thong Yaw Hong.

Tan Sri Dato' Dr Wen Tien Kuang is chairman of Selangor Properties, of which he owns 36%. The company's assets are mostly in the Klang Valley but also include the budget-level Wentworth Hotel in Kuala Lumpur. Selangor used to own Damansara Town Centre but sold out to Kesang Corp.

Dato' Dr Yahaya Bin Ismail runs Cement Industries of Malaysia, part-owned by United Engineers.

Tan Sri Dato' Seri Zain Azraai Bin Zainal Abidin is chairman of Malaysian Airline Systems and of Malaysian Industrial Development Finance.

General Tan Sri Dato' Zain Hashim runs Lion Corp with Tan Sri William Cheng. He is also involved in Klang Securities, Asia Commercial Finance, Silverstone Tire and Rubber, and the Parkson Corporation.

Raja Tan Sri Zainal Bin Raja Sulaiman is the man behind the Pan Malaysia Cement Works.

Tan Sri Dato' Zakaria Bin Haji Mohd Ali is chairman of UMW Holdings Bhd, who remain the sole assembler in Malaysia of Toyota cars. They also have the franchise for Komatsu in Malaysia, Papua New Guinea and the Solomon Islands.

THE PHILIPPINES

Aboitiz, Eduardo and his son, Jon R., run a large and diversified conglomerate involved in agricultural machinery, cargo, electricity and shipping. Jon is president and general manager. The group has strong business interests in both Australia and Norway.

Araneta, Salvador was a partner with Jose Concepcion in the formation of Republic Flour Mills (RFM), the operators forty years ago of South-East Asia's first flour mill. Salvador's daughter married Jose

Jr, who subsequently ran the company before passing it on to his own sons when he joined the government in 1986.

Ayala, Jaime Zobel de is chairman and president of the Ayala group, the largest and most diversified Philippines conglomerate. He also sits on the boards of a number of major local companies, such as Shell Chemical and IBM Philippines. He will be succeeded by his son, Jaime August Zobel de Ayala II, who, like his father, is a Harvard graduate. Don Jaime, as he is known, appears regularly on Forbes' annual billionaire's list.

Brimo, Henry was educated in the United States. He and his son Gerardo run the group which founded the Philex Mining Corporation, a pre-eminent Philippine mining company.

Cojuangco, Antonio O. (known as 'Tony Boy') is, at forty-one years old, president and chief operating officer of the Philippines Long Distance Telephone Company. He is the son of the company's founder, Ramon Cojuangco, and is also a nephew of Corazon Aquino, former president of the Philippines. His great-grandfather was a Chinese immigrant who made his fortune in rice and sugar. An MBA graduate from Stanford, Tony Boy sits on several boards, including those of Kuok Philippines Properties Inc., The Landmark Corporation, and Philippine Airlines. The Cojuangco family is split in business into three distinct factions, of which Tony Boy's is pre-eminent.

Concepcion, Jr III Jose is president and CEO of the Concepcion group, a leading conglomerate which started out in the flour-milling business. He is aided in the day-to-day running of operations by his twin brother Raul and their younger brother Reynaldo. A sister, Eumelia C. Hechanova, is also involved in the business.

Coyiuto, Roberto is chairman of the family company, Prudential Guarantee & Assurance Inc. He also has a controlling interest in Oriental Petroleum and a stake in Alcorn Petroleum, and is an investor in the Manila Chronicle Publishing Corporation. He has been a governor, and chairman and president, of the Manila stock exchange.

Dakay, Benson is the 'seaweed king' of the Philippines. He became a multi-millionaire at the age of 19 through his Shenberg Marketing Corporation.

De Venecia, Oscar, of the Pangasinan family, took over as chairman and president of Basic Petroleum and other family-held companies when his brother, Jose Jr, became speaker of the House of Representatives.

Enrile, Cristina is the wife of Juan Ponce Enrile, a congressman for Cagayan in northern Luzon and a one-time Marcos associate who went on to lead the 1986 People's Power Revolution which brought Corazon Aquino to power. Cristina, together with the couple's children, Jakie and Katrina, runs the family's extensive business interests under their holding company, Jaka Investments Corporation.

Gokongwei, John Jr is probably the richest Filipino-Chinese in the country. He started out with one corn mill and now rules over an empire with involvements in shopping malls and other property, through Robinson Land, in which he has a 60% stake. He is aided in his business by his son, Lance, and his daughter, Robina. He is on the board of Philex, and is also involved with Anscor and the San Miguel Corporation.

Lopez, Eugenio M. Jr is a Harvard Business School graduate whose ancestors made their fortune in sugar about a hundred years ago and then ventured into manufacturing, media and transportation. Eugenio is president of Benpres Corporation and of Manila Chronicle. He works together with his brothers, Oscar M. and Manuel M.

Ramos, Alfredo, or 'Fred', as he is more usually known, runs the family interests in bookstores, communications and property. His personal business involvements include the Philodrill Corporation, one of the most diversified oil exploration companies in the Philippines. He is also a director of Peregrine Capital and Peregrine Securities. He was involved in a fierce but failed hostile takeover battle with the Soriano group for Atlas Consolidated Mining.

Soriano, Andres III is a Wharton School of Finance graduate. He is the eldest son of Don Andres Soriano Jr, and is chairman of the San Miguel Brewery and the San Miguel Corporation. He also runs Anscor, AB Capital and Investment Corporation, Anscor Finance, and La Tondena Distillers. The group holds the regional rights in a number of proprietary brand names, such as Lowenbrau and Kirin. The family are cousins to the Ayala clan.

Sy, Henry is chairman of the Shoemart group of companies, which he runs with the help of his children, Teresita Sy-Coson, Henry Sy Jr, Herbert, Hans, and Harley. He is the Philippines' largest wholesaling and retailing tycoon, through ownership of a number of important shopping malls through the quoted SM Prime Group.

Velayo, Alfredo is one of the Philippines' leading figures in the mining and oil exploration business. As former chairman of the Philodrill Corporation, he is a close associate and business partner of Alfredo Ramos.

Yuchengco, Alfonso T. was the Philippines ambassador to the People's Republic of China under Corazon Aquino, and is head of the family business, which is based on insurance through the Malayan group. His father was the founder in 1930 of China Insurance and Surety, which was later renamed the Malayan Insurance Co. He is helped by his daughter, Helen Yuchengco-Dee, and by his son Alfonso Yuchengco III.

Zobel, Enrique is a cousin of the Soriano family and former vice-chairman of the Ayala corporation. Until ten years ago, he held a major stake in San Miguel. Then he fell out with Don Andres Soriano and sold off his interest to Eduardo Cojuangco. He is nevertheless still involved in projects with the Sorianos and with Kuok Philippine Properties Inc.

SINGAPORE

Chen, Bernard is CEO of INTRACO, which was incorporated in 1968 as a trading company and is 10% owned by Temasek Holdings, 13.8% owned by DBS Bank and 22.4% owned by Natsteel. The company's main purpose is the promotion of exports of locally produced goods and the sourcing of raw materials for local manufacturers.

Dawis, Didi is chairman of QAF, a major food manufacturer and distributor in Malaysia, Thailand and China. The company also owns supermarket operations, including one in Chengdu in China. Nine percent of the company is owned by HRH Prince Mohammed Bolkiah, 18.1% by Watford Investments (HK), 7.1% by China Everbright Holdings and 5.5% by Temasek Holdings.

Fam, Michael is chairman of Carnaud Metalbox Asia Pacific, which took over the assets of the Metalbox Co. of Malaysia in 1975. The company manufactures aluminium and tinplate beverage cans and has investments in Singapore, Thailand, Vietnam, Hong Kong, China and Indonesia. Fam is also chairman of Fraser & Neave, one of the oldest listed companies in Singapore and a leading soft drinks manufacturer and brewer in the region. A subsidiary, Asian-Pacific Breweries, has recently signed agreements to operate breweries in Fuzhou and Bangkok.

Goon Kok Loon is chairman of CWT Distribution, which is partly owned by DBS Bank, the Port of Singapore Authority, INTRACO, and the Jurong Town Corp. The company provides warehousing container depot services, and is Singapore's largest integrated cargo handler.

Howe Yoon Chong is the chairman of Straits Trading, a company founded in 1887 and incorporating Wearne Brothers, a tin smelter. The business, which is 31.4% owned by OCBC, has diversified into other operations through Straits Developments and Killinghall.

Koh Boon Hwee is chairman of Singapore Telecommunications, which has a monopoly on telecommunications and postal services in Singapore. The company is 89.2% owned by Temasek Holdings, but has been a public company since 1993, when it was listed on the Singapore Stock Exchange.

The Kwek/Quek family has branches in Singapore and Malaysia. Eighty-year-old Kwek Hong Png, founder of the Singapore branch's Hong Leong empire, was recently found guilty of helping a nephew commit criminal breach of trust. He could have been sentenced to ten years in prison, but got away with a fine. His eldest son, Kwek Leng Beng, is running the Hong Leong Finance Group. City Developments, the Kweks' property arm, is engaged in building the Republic Plaza in Singapore: when finished, it will be one of the tallest buildings outside the US. In Malaysia, the family is led by Quek Leng Chan. Three years ago, when the Malaysian economy was still recovering from the 1985–6 recession, he invested heavily in manufacturing, property and finance, and profited handsomely. The two branches own stock in each other's holdings but are not close. Quek Leng Chan has said he hopes to make his three main companies as large as today's whole Hong Leong group by the end of the decade. The Kweks were recently worth about $1 billion; the Queks over $700 million.

The Lee family are said to be worth more than $1 billion, based on their interest in the Overseas Chinese Banking Corporation and rubber plantations in Johore. Lee Seng Wee is the taipan.

Lim Hock San is chairman of Singapore Aerospace, part of the defence-related Singapore Technologies (ST) group, incorporated in 1981. The Singapore government has a substantial stake in the company. The group invested $20 million in the start-up of Mobile Aerospace Engineering in the United States.

Lo, Victor is chairman of Gold Peak Industries, which was set up in 1964 for the manufacture of layer-built transistor radios. It is now also involved in electrical wiring fittings and accessories. The company is 27.5% owned by the Lo family.

Lua Cheng Eng is chairman of Jurong Shipyard, a public company and joint venture between Temasek and IHI of Japan. Sembawang Shipyard owns a 16.7% stake.

Ng Pock Too is chairman of Jurong Engineering, which is a joint venture 21.7% owned by the Japanese company Ishikawajima-Harima Heavy Industries and 18.1% owned by Jurong Shipyard. It provides engineering services for power plants, industrial plants, pipelines, storage tanks and communication facilities.

Ong, Beng Seng holds Asian franchises together with his wife Christina and father-in-law Peter Fu, for well-known organisations such as the Hard Rock Café, Planet Hollywood and Haagen Dazs ice cream. He has real estate in the US, Europe and Mexico and is the man behind Singapore's Hotel Properties group which owns the Hilton and the Four Seasons in the city state as well as the Halcyon Hotel in Holland Park in London. He has also launched an airline, Region Air, a credit card operation, the HPL card, an Asian hotel chain Concorde and a cruise line, Taipan Cruises.

Paduka Salehudin Mohamed is involved with Cycle & Carriage, a major force in the Singapore/Malaysia motor trade, with exclusive franchises for Mercedes Benz, Mitsubishi, and Proton in Singapore, and for Mercedes and Mazda in Malaysia. The company is also a non-exclusive distributor of Mitsubishi for Malaysia. It has property investments in the Ampang Hotel Concorde-Malaysia, supermarkets in Malaysia and car franchises in Australia and New Zealand.

Pillay, J. Y. is chairman of Singapore Airlines, which is 53.8% owned by Temasek Holdings, and is one of the largest airlines in the world.

Quek Poh-Huat is president of Singapore Technologies Holdings, which is 100% owned by MOF.

Sim Kee Boon has been chairman for the last ten years of Keppel Corporation, which is 27.4% owned by Temasek. Keppel is one of Singapore's oldest companies, dating back to 1858.

Sim, Wong Hoo is the manufacturer of Singapore's first PC and of the PC sound add-on, Sound Blaster. He set up Creative Technology in 1981 with just $5,000 and is now said to have personal net worth of around $300m.

Tan Boon Teik is chairman of the Singapore Petroleum Company, which is the only independent oil refiner in Singapore. It is part-owned by DBS Bank, Oceanic Petroleum (Asia), Natsteel, the Kuwait Investment Office and Itochu Petroleum. The company is involved in the refining, marketing, distribution and trading of crudes and petroleum products.

Tay, Jannie of the Hour Glass Group started her career as a shoe saleswoman in Australia. Today she is involved in retailing luxury watches and jewellery, and with her Singapore pizza restaurant chain, Milano's.

Teo Ming Kian is chairman of Singapore Technologies Industrial Corporation, the industrial arm of Singapore Technologies Holdings. The company's main business is the manufacture of electronics and IT products and services, precision engineering, construction and development, industrial leasing, travel and leisure, food-processing and distribution, and industrial park development projects with Batam Industrial Park.

Wee, Cho Yaw is chairman of United Overseas Bank, which owns 34% of Haw Par Brothers International, most famous for its Tiger Balm herbal panacea (now controlled by the UOB group). The company dates back to the early 1900s, and was started by two brothers, Aw Boon Haw and Aw Boon Par. It was involved with Slater Walker in the 1970s but now concentrates on pharmaceuticals, sports and leisure, industrial equipment, and investment. It has a 20% stake in Sony Singapore.

Wee, Michael is chairman of Natsteel, which is 16.6% owned by MND Holdings, 16.6% owned by DBS Bank and 17% owned by Temasek Holdings. It is Singapore's only local steel producer, and has also diversified into electronics and resort development (Raffles Marina). The company has a 33.9% joint venture with NatSteel Vina to produce steel in North Vietnam.

Wee Soon Lock, Michael is chairman of Singapore Bus Services, which is 57.6% owned by DBS Nominees (Private). The company, which was incorporated in 1978, runs around 190 bus routes and has a fleet of approximately 2,700 buses. Phua Tin How is MD. There is a property development subsidiary, SingBus Land. A joint venture is in place with the Hanoi Bus Company to assist with the setting up of a public bus service in Vietnam.

Yeo Chee Yeow, Alan is chairman of Rothmans Industries, which was originally incorporated in 1979 as Gunston Tobacco. It is now an investment holding company, with subsidiaries in manufacturing and the import and distribution of tobacco and tobacco-related products.

Yeo, Philip is chairman of Sembawang Corporation, whose subsidiaries are involved in construction, steel fabrication, aviation services, financial services and property development.

TAIWAN

Chang, Y. F. and family own 15.97% of Evergreen Marine, part of the Evergreen group, one of Taiwan's fastest-growing consortiums. Started in 1968, Evergreen Marine is the world's second largest container shipper, after Maersk of Denmark, and commands a number one market share on the round-the-world and transpacific routes. The group also owns a large interest in Eva Airlines, which runs planes along the lucrative Taiwan-Hong Kong, and Taiwan-Japan routes.

Chen, Yuhao and family run the Tuntex group, Taiwan's third largest property developer and fifth largest polyester fibre manufacturer. They have also diversified into hotel management and own 55% of The Regent Hotel, one of Taiwan's most prestigious hotel properties.

Chiao, Yucheng is taipan of one of Taiwan's leading wire and cable producers, Walsin Lihwa. Of all Taiwanese listed companies, it is the leading investor in mainland China, with four projects up and running.

Chou, Mrs Yinhsi is chairman of Chung Shing Textile, owner of one of Taiwan's most profitable department stores, Sunrise, and the widow of the late C. Y. Baw, who founded the company in 1949. Mrs Chou is concentrating on expanding the business overseas to take advantage of low-cost production in mainland China and Vietnam.

Hsu, Hsutung and family own 25% of Far Eastern Textile, a fifty-year-old company which started life in Shanghai and has expanded into construction, financial services, tourism and chemicals. The group is under the leadership of Douglas Hsu, eldest son of the founder.

Hsu, Shuchen is chairman of his family conglomerate, which has close ties with a number of Japanese corporations, including Mitsubishi Electric and Yokohama Rubber. The company started out half a century ago in trucking, but today embraces electrical goods manufacture (Shihlin Electric), tyres (Nan Kang Tire), transport (Shinchu Island Transportation) and the Ambassador Hotel in Taipei.

Kao, Chin-yen founded The President Group in 1967, together with the current chairman, Wu Hsiuchi. The conglomerate started out in flour-milling and now has ambitions to be the world's biggest food group within the next twenty-five years. They own the 7-11 franchise in Taiwan, and Famous Amos cookies (US). Kao has expanded heavily into China and plans to take on the US market next. He is a member of the 'Tainan Gang', a powerful local business network, and chairman of the ROC Federation of Industry.

Koo, Chenfu is chairman of his family operations in Taiwan, the Philippines and Hong Kong. There are three flagship companies, Taiwan Cement, Chinatrust Bank and China Life Insurance.

Lin, Teng and family own Goldsun (formerly Kuo Chan), a small conglomerate dealing in concrete, construction and property development, and Taiwan Secom, a maker and supplier of security products and services. They are also involved in Taiwan's largest supplier of tissue paper, through Taiwan Scott Paper, and in Trans-Asia Airways.

Miau, Matthew (Feng Chian) of Mitac Computers has current sales of around $2bn per annum. Miau worked for Intel for several years and became a Taiwanese distributor for their products before starting Mitac about 20 years ago. He also has interests in Lien Hua Industrial Gases and in Union Petrochemical.

Oung, James (Da Ming) is the eldest son of the late Ming Chang Oung, founder of Hualon Teijran. He was recently embroiled in a fracas with the company related to possible stock fraud. The group is involved in a wide area of business, including trade, textiles, insurance (Kuo Hua Life Insurance), construction and securities. Oung has recently diversified into electronics with a new venture, the Hi-Sincerity Microelectronics Corporation.

Shih, Stanley (Chenjung) runs Acer, which started life in 1981 and is today one of Taiwan's pre-eminent computer companies. It recently merged with the American company, Altos.

Show, Shen Ho and his brother, *Show, Chung Ho* started the Yuen Foong Yu Paper Manufacturing company in 1945. It is now Taiwan's largest paper company. Also involved in the business is another taipan, T. J. Hung. Both families are closely connected to the Kuomintang. The company has expanded into the financial, computer and venture capital sectors, and internationally into both Thailand and China.

Sun, David, the eldest son of *Sun, Fa-Min*, the leader of the Pacific Group of Companies with 40 businesses in retail, telecommunications, hotels, finance and entertainment. Other families involved in Pacific are the Chiaos and Lees.

Tsai, Hungtu and his family run the Lin Yuan conglomerate, Taiwan's largest in terms of assets, which is made up of Cathay Life, Cathay Trust and Fubon Insurance. The Tsais also have a controlling interest in Taiwan First Investment Trust.

Wang, Yu Yun, a former policeman and mayor, formed Hua, Eng W & C with his brother in 1956. It is now the largest optical cable maker in Taiwan. Wang Senior was a presidential adviser and was also chairman of the Commission of National Corporations. He is succeeded by his Western-educated son, Wang Chih-Shun, also a legislator. They have recently set up the Chung Hsing Bank.

Wang, Yung-ching and family run the forty-year old Formosa Plastics empire, Taiwan's largest private consortium, which includes Formosa Chemicals, Formosa Taffeta and Nan Ya Plastics. The dynasty includes Cher, Winston and Charlene, who help to run several divisions of the group.

Wang, Yutseng, his four sons and the rest of the family own the

China Rebar group, which started out in 1959 manufacturing steel for construction. They have since expanded into textiles and engineering, and on into department stores and hotels. The five-star Rebar Hotel in Taipei is one of their properties, and the group also has a fifteen-year franchise with Holiday Inn.

Wu, Tungching and his family own 55% of the Shinkong group, which is involved in textiles and insurance. They have also diversified into securities, with Taiwan Securities, a joint venture with S. G. Warburg, Nomura Securities and Sanyo Securities. The group has a further interest in the Taishin Bank.

Yen, Vivian W. is chairman of Yue Loong Motor Company, which was born of an association between Tai Yuen Textiles and Nissan and Mitsubishi, and is one of Taiwan's largest sellers of cars. Mrs Yen is said to be planning diversification into the financial sector and land development.

Yin, Yenliang is a professor at Cheng Chi University and National Taiwan University, and is the second-generation taipan of the Runtex Textile group, founded by his father, the late Yin Shu-Tien. The company is also involved in the Kwang Hwa Securities Investment Trust Corporation and in the Grand Cathay Securities Company.

THAILAND

Asavabhokhin, Anant owns a chunk of Bangkok's Mandarin Hotel and is chairman of Land & Houses, the market leader and most reputable of Thailand's companies in the residential housing sector. Also involved in the construction and finance sectors, Anant is considered to be the country's property whizzkid.

Chakkapak, Pin is probably Thailand's pre-eminent takeover taipan. He heads Finance One and the so-called One Group, which began life in the 1920s. He is involved today in a joint venture with C. P. Pokhphand, the Thai Farmers' Bank and the French bank, Paribas. Pin recently secured a 15% stake in the Bank of Asia.

Chearavanont, Dhanin and family control C. P. Pokhphand, the most internationally aggressive of all Thai conglomerates, whose main business lies in the agricultural sector. The company has diversified widely into manufacturing, petrochemicals, retail, and telecommunications. It is likely that Dhanin's brother, Sumet, will succeed him.

Chokwatana, Boonsithi is the third son of Thiam, the founder of Saha Pathanapibul, the largest Thai distributor of basic consumer goods. The company is mainly involved in shoes, textiles and food-processing, and the family also have interests in developing industrial parks, in which they work closely with the Japanese. Boonsithi is likely to be followed in the business by his younger brother, Boonchai.

Horrungruang, Sawasdi is master of the NTS Steel Group. He works in tandem with his heir apparent, Chamni Chanchai. What started out as a small trading firm spilled over into manufacturing about twenty years ago, and then into the development of industrial estates. Sawasdi is said to be close to the government, and he is certainly highly influential in shaping the country's steel policy.

Kanjanapas, Mongkol built Bangkok Land and Tanayong from a humble watch shop into broadcasting, finance, hotels, property, and property assets. The founder's two children, Anand and Keeree, run Bangkok Land and Tanayong respectively. The family are closely involved with the Ratanaraks and a number of other Sino-Thais.

Lamsam, Banthoon is involved with Loxley a conglomerate owning significant interests in, among other things, telecommunications (representatives of foreign armaments manufacturers) and the Thai Farmers' Bank. The latter is the third largest bank in the country and was founded by Choti Lamsam, in 1945. The family have close links with the military.

Laohathai, Sawang heads the Metro Group, a distributor of agricultural chemicals. Through a subsidiary, the company is involved in fertiliser and plastic storage bags. Sawang is considered a member of the Sino-Thai 'top circle' in Thailand, and is very close to the Sophonpanich clan. Laohathai's heir apparent is said to be a fellow director, Plengsak Prakatphesat.

Osathanugrah, Surat is the second son of the founder of the Premier

Group, Sawasdi, who will be succeeded at the helm by his nephew, Thana Chaiprasu. The group is involved in pharmaceuticals and consumer products and the financial sector.

Phongsathorn, Vichien is a relative of the Osathanugrah family and is presently in charge of their Premier Group subsidiary, Premier Enterprise, which is involved in pharmaceuticals and chemicals. The parent company also has a stake in First Pacific Land. The founder of the original company was Sawasdi Osathanugrah, who was succeeded by Sawasdi, his second son. He in turn will be followed by his nephew, Thana Chaiprasit. This main part of the family runs the financial services-related business.

Ratanarak, Krit runs the Bank of Ayudhya and is the son of the group's founder, Chuan, who died in 1993. Although the bank is the group's pivotal company, there are insurance, broadcasting and television subsidiaries, as well as the Siam City Cement group, which was started in 1969 and has since expanded its activities into the manufacture of a number of other building materials.

Shinawatra, Dr Thaksin and his wife, Potjaman, own Shinawatra Computer & Communications, which is both a holding company and a computer- and communications-related business trading in IBM mainframes and AT&T and NCR equipment. Shinawatra's money came from silk – his family owned one of the nation's largest silk companies. A former policeman, Thaksin would like to see the company become a regional telecommunications giant.

Sophonpanich, Chatri, the politically well-connected son of the late Chin Sophonpanich, is the pre-eminent Thai taipan. He controls the Bangkok Bank group, which was founded by his father. Chatri's children, Chatsiri, Chali and Sawitree, run Bangkok Bank, the City Realty property arm and Asia Securities Trading, and Union Asia Finance respectively.

Chapter 8

Mind-Mapping the Taipans

(i) GREATER CHINA

In order to understand the business dealings of the new taipans, it is essential to be familiar with their turf. There is very little about the cities of Asia or the way people conduct their daily lives there that is familiar to the West. The key factor is speed: speed of thought, speed of decision-making and speed of commercial action. Everything is done at least twice as fast as it would be even in New York. Time waits for no one and lucrative business deals have to be made yesterday or the day before, not tomorrow. The concept of 'insider information' is an alien one: there is no such thing in Asia. Those who are on the outside are simply not in business. All commercial knowledge is disseminated through the 'guanxis' and acted upon more or less in concert. A journalist once described Hong Kong as 'an institutionalised nonsense, an argy-bargy', but the chaos there has produced some of the world's greatest success stories.

The seeds of a new economic world order are being planted in the Far East, and nowhere more so than in China and Hong Kong. For the first time, the world can see that China may now begin to achieve an economic significance commensurate with her demographic and political weight. And while China is vital to Hong Kong's immediate fate, Hong Kong holds the key to China's long-term future. Hong Kong and Taiwan constitute two very willing providers of capital and expertise on China's coastline. Both already have successful investment track records, and they effectively control the economies of two of China's most successful regions, Guangdong and Fujian.

Hong Kong Island was ceded to Britain, under the 1842 Treaty of Nanking, as spoils from the Opium War. The Kowloon Peninsula was acquired by the British in 1860, and the New Territories were secured on a ninety-nine-year lease from 1898. It is that lease that is about to expire. The mighty, mostly Scottish taipans lived on the Peak, from where they administered the considerable opium-backed riches of their conglomerates, the 'hongs'.

It was, however, communism not colonialism that had the greatest impact on Hong Kong, when, with the 1949 Revolution and the fall of Shanghai, a wave of refugee industrialists relocated their fortunes to the territory. No city in the world has ever grown more quickly in population, in stature, in wealth. Today, Hong Kong sits at GATT meetings as the world's sixteenth largest trading economy. Its six million inhabitants produce and export more goods and services than India's 625 million.

It is said that the business scene in Hong Kong is like a game of tennis at the Ladies' Recreation Club: everyone plays with and knows each other, and all have a thorough work-out. The tremendous advantage of the closed-shop nature of the commercial set is the opportunity it affords the taipans repeatedly to take parts of their empires public, and in so doing to pull a seemingly endless succession of companies out of their hats. The definitions of public and private are very blurred, but one thing is certain: when an asset reaches the public, the best bits have already been dealt out to friends.

Nowadays, the players may be changing, but the game is fundamentally the same. The taipans' new business partners, apart from those from the People's Republic, are the Japanese, who have been very large investors in Hong Kong in recent years. There are Japanese department stores, construction companies, manufacturers, and, of course, banks. The Americans are also a major presence: AT&T and IBM have both switched their Asian headquarters from Tokyo to Hong Kong.

The area that has now come to be known as 'Greater China' is potentially the most valuable of all of the taipans' Pacific Rim domains. The successful coastal economies of Japan, South Korea, Hong Kong and Singapore are turning to their populous, land-rich but capital-starved neighbour for expansion into the next century. This has created a Greater China economy, or a China bloc. Once the profit motive is present, the Chinese work ethic hurtles through like a runaway train. Forty years of stultifying totalitarianism was not enough to kill it off. When hope replaces the weary depression which blights most people in China, the potential is staggering.

There is no doubt that the momentum for a Greater China is part of a wider series of developments which are taking place today all over Asia. It is as if those apparently crippling historical and political barriers are being bulldozed by economic imperatives, above all, the need to maintain a competitive edge in the face of rising costs. The area must also diversify away from dependence on the US as its main market, a requirement which has never been more important. The governments in Taipei and Beijing have accommodated themselves to these developments with much less reluctance than might have been expected.

The volume of commercial traffic between Hong Kong and China is enormous: it is estimated that 10,000 vehicles use the Man Kam crossing point – just one of many – each day. There are now more than two and a half million people in China employed by Hong Kong manufacturers, although it is hard to keep count. This compares with only 800,000 manufacturing employees in the whole of Hong Kong itself. The Bank of China, with its twelve associated institutions, is now wholly owned by the People's Republic. It is Hong Kong's second largest high-street bank, and its cash cards interface with those of Britain's Standard Chartered.

The new economic community of the region consists of Hong Kong, Macau, Guangdong, Taiwan and Fujian, and has an aggregate population of 120 million people and an aggregate GDP in the region of $200 billion. That makes it considerably bigger than Australia. While Hong Kong per se of course plays a pivotal role, it is the emergence of the territory as an engine of growth which counts.

The enormous amount of trade done so far in the 1990s, despite the continuance of a long-standing Communist regime, is a testament to the ability of business to make politics irrelevant. The power behind that business is none other than that of the taipans. Few doubt that without their impetus the People's Republic would not be moving in its present business direction. The 'colonisation' of areas of China will continue, and is already embracing Shanghai and other major cities. There is no doubt that this is a far more important influence on the future of the region than any short-term political problems. The trends are unstoppable because the decisions for change are taken in the boardroom, not by politicians. David Li, CEO of the Bank of East Asia, has estimated that investment in the

China/Taiwan/Hong Kong triangle is now reaching an annual rate of $6 billion.

Taiwan is very much more than a mere adjunct to the Greater China economy. However, because her commercial star has risen somewhat more belatedly than that of Hong Kong, her taipans have been less than visible, even to those who know the country well. The fortunes of Taiwan's taipans have largely been made as a result of their role as commercial intermediaries. The legacy of years as a Japanese colony has been the creation of a highly efficient and well-ordered, if overly bureaucratic, environment that runs commercial enterprises without a hitch. The place that started out manufacturing cheap imitations of high-priced goods has now metamorphosed into a much more sophisticated market with a highly demanding and wealthy consumer mass.

Nine out of ten of Taiwan's businesses are small, family-owned organisations, who together are responsible for 41% of the country's total output. It is from these family businesses that large conglomerates with complex shareholding structures and alliances have grown. Taipans like Wang Yung-ching, C. F. Koo and Chang Yung-fa are outstanding examples of this progress, and are all key figures in both economic and political circles.

Despite his vast wealth, Wang Yungching has an austere and spartan life, shunning all obvious shows of materialism. He is even said to refuse to spend money on new clothes, to such an extent that his wife has to copy his old favourites and surreptitiously replace them, without him noticing, before they fall apart. He is one of the few taipans who did not come from humble beginnings, but was born in Taipei to a landed family who were dispossessed as part of the country's land reform programme. It was the compensation received for this loss that allowed him to go into business. A chronic workaholic of the most impassioned kind, Wang hates to waste time. The only indulgence he will allow himself is the occasional swim or round of golf. He has been known to jog, considering that the most convenient, inexpensive and immediate of all sports.

Wang, together with his younger brother, Y. T. Wang, and Y. T.'s two sons and six daughters, owns and oversees the Formosa Plastics group. The company has nearly 2,000 employees and is said to be worth $2.5 billion. The company has just completed work on Texas's most expensive construction project ever, a $2.1 billion petrochemical and plastics manufacturing compound. Wang started out in 1957 producing just four tons of plastic each day; today that figure has risen to something around the 800,000 tonnes mark. The by-products of the process have led to the manufacture of a whole range of products, from shock absorbers to furniture.

Wang also owns 10% of Formosa Taffeta, 25% of Formosa Chemicals, 9.4% of Formosa Plastics and 15% of Nan Ya Plastics. He is far and away the richest man in Taiwan. Lately he has been spending his days in Florham Park, New Jersey, overseeing Formosa Plastics' American operations. The Wangs are the most powerful overseas investors in the US petrochemical industry and have around eight plants in various locations.

Wang's personal philosophy has always been to work as hard as is humanly possible and to make sure that life is one long continuous learning process. He maintains that in business one should never take any situation at face value. He has always prided himself on being perfectly prepared for the unexpected. He is grateful that the loss of his family's inheritance provided him with the opportunity to create an altogether far more important source of riches. His parsimony has paid dividends, especially in his canny bargaining ability, which has enabled him to obtain discounts on the raw materials, such as salt from Australia, that his business requires.

Chang Yung-fa, together with his family, owns 15.97% of Evergreen Marine. This is the core of the Evergreen group, one of Taiwan's fastest-growing consortiums, which was founded in 1968. The company is now the world's second largest container shipper, with fifty-four ships. Evergreen Marine also owns 26.67% of Eva Airlines, a property that is becoming increasingly burdensome but now has twenty aircraft.

Nearly in the same league are the Koo family who own Taiwan Cement. Their business has gradually diversified overseas and into other fields: China Life Insurance is Taiwan's fifth largest life insurer; the Chinatrust Bank became a commercial bank in 1992 and now has twenty-two branches on the island and four overseas representative offices.

Taiwan can also boast the Tsai family, who own the Lin Yuan conglomerate. They have control of the vast Cathay group with interests in insurance, private banking and the building industry, through Cathay Life, Cathay Trust, Cathay Property Insurance and Cathay Construction. A promising company always looks over its shoulder to see if the Tsais are about to pop up and take it over.

One of the largest conglomerates on the island, however, consisting of 102 different companies, is owned not by taipans but by the Kuomintang, Taiwan's ruling political party. Historically, the Kuomintang have been allowed to operate monopoly businesses and make very large profits, without necessarily having to be good businessmen. Recent deregulation, though, has opened up a whole new territory for the taipans to poach and run along their more efficient lines. The greatest challenge to be faced by the taipans of Taiwan in the next few years is the formulation of strategies towards mainland China.

The phenomenon that is taking place in Greater China generally is none other than the highly successful recycling of so-called expo-dollars, in much the same way as the oil-producing countries recycled their petrodollars in the 1970s. The Japanese attempted the same feat in the 1980s through a property and corporate spending spree, but it was for the most part largely ill advised and ended in disaster. The taipans are both more canny and more worldly. The other main difference is that the size of the export of capital by Hong Kong and Taiwan to China threatens to dwarf that of the rest of the world put together.

Perhaps the most astonishing of the Hong Kong taipans' companies – and certainly the most surprising of the taipans – is CITIC and its CEO Larry Yung. An engineer by training, Yung spent most of the Cultural Revolution pouring concrete in a remote part of China. CITIC is the one corporate vehicle that all the other taipans must now hinge on – if only for appearances' sake – until the political future of mainland China is clear. The company, in which Beijing has a 49% stake, was set up in Hong Kong in 1980 as the first major corporate Chinese mainland presence, and was ostensibly formed to attract funds and technology to China. In 1985 it was incorporated under the name of Tylfull and a year later took over the listing of Sun King Fung Development Ltd. The shareholders are a more than averagely interesting bunch. Chief amongst them is Li Ka-Shing, the taipan's taipan; Robert Kuok of the Shangri-la Group, Kerry and the SCMP; Peregrine Investments, a K. S. Li vehicle headed up by Englishman Philip Tose; and the Chao family, the previous owners of the controlling interest in Tylfull. By the end of 1989 CITIC had approved investments worth about $2 billion in around ninety countries. The combination of these personalities, their wealth and their connections is unstoppable.

As Victor Fung, the chairman of investment bank Prudential Asia, says, 'For a new partnership, a personal reference from a respected member of the Chinese business community is worth more than any amount of money you could throw on the table.' Fung and his brother William, who are both Harvard MBAs, are the new generation of the Li and Fung families, one of the oldest Hong Kong trading dynasties, who now spend most of their time in venture capital.

There is nothing the taipans cannot or will not do to set China on the right commercial track, and benefit their own companies in the process. In October 1987, for example, Ronald Li, the founder and chairman of the Hong Kong Stock Exchange, suspended trading there for four days rather than see his own fortune diluted in the crash. He was sentenced to four years in prison for his part in a related stock fraud. Keen businessmen have even pushed to the backs of their minds the bloody events of June 1989 in Tiananmen Square – despite the fact that at the time a million people took to the streets of Hong Kong in protest.

Whilst anything could happen in this alliance between capitalist colony and Communist mainland, plans have been laid to fill the vacuum after 1997. Universal suffrage is to be introduced. A third of legislative councillors are to be directly elected, and appointed members will be phased out completely over time. The executive council will remain the most powerful body, and will be appointed by a chief executive, who will replace the Governor in 1997. This appointment will be ratified by Beijing instead of the Queen.

Many businessmen in Hong Kong today argue that it is wrong of people in the democracies of the West to compare Hong Kong and China with anything in their experience. Hong Kong has had less than two hundred years of education and democratic traditions. The taipans cite, for example, the fact that the West has a substantial trade union movement which, Hong Kong people believe, controls certain industries and limits prosperity. Hong Kong, on the other hand, has the freedom to hire and fire. Every day is a personal testing ground.

According to *Asiaweek*, the top companies in Hong Kong in the 1990s are the Hong Kong & Shanghai Bank, China Light & Power, HK Telecommunications, Cathay Pacific, Mass Transit Railway Corporation, and Hutchison Whampoa. The list in fact gives an erroneous impression of a Hong Kong still largely run by expatriate-dominated conglomerates with at least five decades' worth of history behind them. Nothing could be further from the truth. The power now lies with a group of taipans whose influence stems from the synergy of the old with the new.

CITIC's Larry Yung is one of Greater China's richest men, and perhaps the ultimate in the PRC's new taipans. He is also the son of Rong Yiren, a Deng Xiaoping intimate who founded CITIC and who was until quite recently its chairman. It is this nepotism perhaps that accounts for the fact that CITIC is answerable not to its nominal ministry (as is the case with other state-run enterprises), but directly to the State Council, China's cabinet. This in effect gives CITIC the position of a ministry, and therefore makes Yung a *de facto* minister, while at the same time he lives the life of Riley in Hong Kong. On a day-to-day basis, there is no direct interference in CITIC from Beijing. Nor need there be, because as long as they continue with their present success, intervention of any kind could only impede their stunning progress. In a very short time, CITIC has become a highly lucrative and intensely capitalist corporation. Its Communist parents can only be astonished at their latent capitalist zeal and wonder why they have wasted the last forty-five years.

Besides its involvement in trading, distribution, infrastructural development, banking, and foreign exchange, one further indication of just how much the PRC is prepared to bend its ideology to accommodate capitalism (especially where personal gain might be involved) is its 20% ownership through CITIC of the Manhattan Card Co. Ltd. Formerly Chase Manhattan Bank's credit card operation in Hong Kong, this has been since 1993 a separate company, and is now one of the leading issuers, marketeers and service companies in the territory of premium and standard credit cards.

CITIC now also owns a percentage of Dah Chong Hong (a local trading house specialising in the distribution of motor vehicles and accessories); a stake in Swire with 12.5% of Cathay Pacific; 38% of Dragonair (Hong Kong's second passenger airline, flying to twelve destinations in China and five elsewhere in Asia); HACTL; 30% of Hong Kong Telecom; 20% of CTM, the Macau telephone company; Hongkong Resort; three power stations in China; Sent Waste Management; and a waste treatment plant in Hong Kong. All this as well as significant infrastructural development interests in the Western Harbour Crossing, the Eastern Harbour Crossing Rail and Road, and the Shanghai Tunnel. In 1991, Li Ka-Shing and Philip Tose,

CEO of Peregrine, acquired minority shares in CITIC through the purchase of convertible bonds issued to finance the acquisition of Cathay Pacific, CTM, and Hang Chong, a company involved in the sale of cars, lorries and buses.

CITIC entities also control the second biggest retail banking network in Hong Kong, and half of the Chinese merchant shipping fleet, owned and operated out of Hong Kong by China Merchants' Steam Navigation Co. – an offshoot of the Ministry of Communications in Beijing. Another entity, the China Resources Corporation, controls the wholesale trade in nearly all of the food going in and out of China. It is as if CITIC were designed simply to boost the confidence of Hong Kong businessmen in life after 1997 by showing them that China can play them at their own game. CITIC is now one of the colony's biggest investors.

Yung is not the only significant mainland player in Hong Kong. A number of former Communist leaders are all dabbling in the ways of Mammon, with the result that the number of Hong Kong businesses now controlled by Chinese state-owned companies has risen in a short time from 400 to 1,000. The precise number of openly state-owned Chinese companies listed in Hong Kong stands at forty-seven, accounting for 7% of total market capitalisation. The red has turned a much whiter shade of pink. A great deal of this might possibly be due to a kind of laundering, but of assets rather than cash. One of the only ways of turning state assets into lucre is by taking back-door listings, or by bringing the company to the market and using Hong Kong to book profits from artificially deflated export prices.

Li Ka-Shing – who is increasingly referred to in Hong Kong simply as K. S. Li – has been a very great help to the People's Republic of China, which is no doubt why they hold him in such high esteem. From modest beginnings, his became one of the fastest-blossoming fortunes in Hong Kong history. Only forty years ago, he used to earn $12 a month in a plastic flower factory. Now he is officially estimated to have a personal net worth of about $5 billion. His stake in Cheung Kong alone is worth $3.5 billion at today's prices. He is involved, directly or indirectly, with a number of 'red-chip' companies such as Shougang Holdings, and through them with Deng Xiaoping's younger son, Deng Zhifang. He helped Shougang and First Shanghai Investment to secure back-door listings and to make a series of ambitious takeover bids.

117

Li's immense investment in China has won him the distinction of being dubbed a patriot by Chinese premier Li Peng, yet he staunchly declares that he is not, contrary to all appearances, pro-Beijing. He was a great friend of the late Sir Y. K. Pao, a relationship which has not lasted through to Pao's son-in-law and successor, Peter Woo. Woo, who used to work for Chase Manhattan Bank, is now very busy making his mark as chairman of Hong Kong's Wheelock Marden Group. He has $12 billion worth of assets to play with, including a fine property portfolio which comprises shopping centres in Beijing, Dalien and Shanghai, and the construction contract for Hong Kong's new cross-harbour tunnel. An MBA graduate of Columbia University, Woo has recently formalised commercial relationships with the Australian brewery company, Fosters; and with Britain's Virgin group, to open record stores around the region.

There are always a lot of theories doing the rounds in Hong Kong about Deng Xiao Ping's family. Unsurprisingly, it seems that they are concerned about a possible backlash against them when Deng dies, and his daughter has been buying apartments in Singapore to use as boltholes in the event of such a reaction. The power struggle that will doubtless follow his demise will result in a rapid shifting of alliances that will probably take their toll in the market. An example of this was the arrest of the chairman of Shougang, even though one of Deng Xiao Ping's sons was on the board. One of the more interesting 'red chip' companies, China Venturetech, is run by the daughter of a senior Communist, Chen Weili. And T. T. Tsui, a potential first chief executive of Hong Kong post-1997, runs the government-dominated New China Hongkong group. Tsui, an avid collector of Chinese artefacts, was the sponsor of the new Oriental Gallery in London's Victoria & Albert museum, and is also the owner of the T. T. Tsui Museum on the first floor of the old Bank of China building. The American company, Goldman Sachs, has a stake in Tsui's New China group, as do Li Ka-Shing and Stanley Ho. Even the army is cashing in, with a share in Norinco, a munitions manufacturer.

Li Ka-Shing is perfectly positioned to wield massive influence in the China of tomorrow. He is on the PRC Preliminary Working Committee, Beijing's advisory board for Hong Kong, together with Robert Kuok, a Malaysian entrepreneur and his partner in the Beijing World Trade Centre. Li's eldest son, Victor, keeps the political balance with a seat on Governor Chris Patten's Business Council that was intended for Li himself. He nominated Victor to take his place, perhaps to indicate the seriousness of his son's role in the family operations. Li and Kuok are joined on the PRC committee by Chatri Sophonpanich, president of Bangkok Bank, Thailand's largest listed company, which recently opened up in China. Other corporate allies include Gordon Wu, Henry Fok, Stanley Ho, C. P. Yu and Dennis Ting. Raymond Chow of Golden Harvest is a regular golf partner.

Friends and family, the consistently most important of Chinese values, once again dominate. What may appear to the outsider to be a sort of ganging up in business of Oriental against white man is very much more complex when scrutinised. In the mid-1980s, for example, the well-known lawyer, Robert Wang, was much celebrated for his commercial achievement in bringing together a number of the Hong Kong elite for a Singapore property venture, Suntech. The eight wealthy Hong Kong families involved were all connected of old from Shanghai and had a natural alliance that went back for generations. To those familiar with such arrangements, their union made perfect sense.

Even if Chinese businessmen do not have family or political connections with those they deal with, they all at least share a passion for new business and the old ways of China. Li Ka-Shing is buoyantly optimistic that some good will come out of all these changes. 'The Chinese are not fools,' he has said. 'Sooner or later a country like China must find the right direction.' Even so, he is seriously considering shifting his group's legal headquarters out of Hong Kong. He is also pumping money into a big commercial complex in Singapore and actively shopping for more acquisitions in the West. Nevertheless, politics takes second place. It is much more straightforward here to be a successful businessman than a successful politician. The winds of business fortune are considerably easier to second-guess than those of politics.

Li, in common with most Chinese, is deeply superstitious. He will not even strike the ground with a shovel without spending hours in consultation with the 'feng shui' man, whose geomancy is essential to make sure that any project's design and physical placement pass muster with the local spirit population. That is how the waterfront Regent Hotel (not owned by Li) ended up with panoramic floor-to-ceiling windows the full length of its lobby: the nine invisible dragons of Kowloon had to be guaranteed ease of passage when they needed a drink. And business at the hotel has boomed from the start. In the same vein, the mighty Aberdeen power station was built with five chimneys, rather than the more usual four. Four is the unluckiest of all numbers, denoting death, and can only mean very bad 'feng shui'. One of the chimneys was in fact just a dummy, which was subsequently knocked down to make way for the Ap Lei Chau housing development – a Cheung Kong group deal, of course, since it was a Hong Kong Electric power station.

The spectre of 1997 now looms a short time away. The stakes being played for are the six million inhabitants of the colony, who are destined in any case to become a minor subset of the population of China. There are, it is true, those who have left vowing never to return; and there are also those who left and have already returned, having established residency in far-off lands, just in case. If all goes well, Hong Kong will merely continue smoothly along its capitalist course. After all, the 1984 Sino-British Declaration, which promised that Her Majesty's Government would hand the British colony over to Beijing, contained the stipulation that Hong Kong's lifestyle and economic system should remain untouched for fifty years. With its proposed 'one country, two systems', China has effectively promised to try an experiment that would be dismissed anywhere else as unworkable.

Many people believe that Hong Kong should not even have survived this far. There is no semblance of welfare, of societal paternalism, or protection for the weak; no safety net of any kind. Taxes are low, the government is to all intents and purposes non-interventionist, the bureaucracy is efficient without being intrusive and the infrastructure is second to none. These factors, allied with the Chinese obsession for work, make Hong Kong the best of all possible places for business. The result is a free-for-all in which millionaires rise and fall on an almost yearly basis. The marriage of this unconstrained society with the extreme interventionism of what is still, to all purposes, a Marxist-Leninist state can only give birth to the most extraordinary of children.

Property is probably more important in Asia than anywhere else, forming as it does the cornerstone of every successful commercial portfolio. Some 60% of corporate assets are held in the form of real estate. Even after a major slump, assets are traded rather than kept as an investment. The property boom that started in the early eighties still has not stalled. Rents have skyrocketed in both the commercial and the residential sectors. Demand has grown to such an extent that new expatriates moving to take advantage of the Hong Kong wave now dread that their lot will be to live in a shack out on the islands of Lamma or Cheung Chau. Recently even the New Territories have become very expensive because of the massive infrastructural development that is taking place and because of the region's proximity to China.

Most Westerners first became aware of Li Ka-Shing as the Hong Kong billionaire who was keeping the wolf from the door of the Canadian Reichmanns over Canary Wharf. Up till then, few outside the territory had even known of his existence. Li made his fortune in property and trading, and for over a decade now has been diversifying abroad, into Singapore and North America. At home he is held in very high regard: in a newspaper poll, he was voted Hong Kong's most popular figure, well ahead of Governor Chris Patten.

He is thought to be the fourth richest person in Asia, behind the Sultan of Brunei and Japanese property tycoons Minoru Mori and Toichi Takenaka. His commercial portfolio, which includes Cheung Kong, Hutchison Whampoa and its associates, now accounts for 15% of the capitalisation of the Hong Kong Stock Exchange. Despite his vast wealth, he has kept his original office, a distinctly unimpressive building. It is typical of a taipan not to want to let go of a property that has brought him very good 'feng shui'. He still lives in a spacious but sparsely furnished house in Deepwater Bay that he bought for HK$100,000 three decades ago. His money today would allow him to buy or build the very best that the world has to offer.

Cheung Kong, Li Ka-Shing's flagship company, has experienced unprecedented growth in the past twenty years, on the back of both robust economic conditions in Hong Kong and Li's own uncanny foresight. Cheung Kong acts as a merchant banker, participating in venture capital, fund management, securities trading and corporate finance. The group is an invaluable partner in venture capital funds investing in China, and its huge financial clout makes it a prominent player in the Hong Kong market. Li makes sure that all his business is kept under tight financial control. Much of his mergers-and-acquisitions manoeuvring is done through CEF Holdings, a joint venture he has with the Canadian Imperial Bank of Commerce. Almost all his stockbroking and related activity is conducted through Peregrine Brokerage, a consortium co-owned by most of the colony's well-heeled taipans and with a small stake also held by China. The market value of Li's investment in Hong Kong, through all the many arms of his octopus-like empire, has grown to around $9.2 billion, with an unrealised profit of $3 billion.

Every commercial move that Li Ka-Shing makes is scrutinised and dissected by everyone in Hong Kong from car park attendants to fellow billionaires. In this way, the average punter hopes to identify for himself those economic trends that might be useful for his own personal strategy. Li has only to breathe in the general direction of a new wave and thousands of investors will follow him. No other man is more capable of causing alarming disturbances in the stock market.

In Hong Kong, Li is seen as the very embodiment of the new Asian Dream, held in an esteem that other businessmen and women can only envy. He discusses business round the clock quite happily, but will hardly ever talk to members of the press. He knows that every time he says something about business, the economy, or the stock market, there will be some sort of reaction, and that reaction will not always be favourable. Li says he always tries to forge his business alliances by being a 'little bit more than fair'. No one gets to be that powerful, however, without having upset a few people along the way, and he managed to arouse considerable debate recently with some very controversial options in Cheung Kong, which prompted the *Far Eastern Review* headline: 'Cashing in, the Cheung Kong way'.

Li's career began when he left school at the age of fourteen and supported his mother, sister and younger brother by selling fake flowers as a street-hawker. By the time he was twenty-two, this modest business had blossomed into a major plastics factory. Five years later, he started Cheung Kong, which was incorporated in 1971 and floated the following year, and from there it was but a small jump to tycoon. Two-thirds of Li's ability probably lies in analysis of the shrewdest, most hard-nosed kind, and the other third in unbelievable intuition. His big break was handed to him by Michael Sandberg, the then chairman of the Hongkong & Shanghai Bank. In 1979, the bank sold him its 22.8% stake in Hutchison, which made Li the first Chinese to control one of five traditionally British hongs in Hong Kong. Simon Murray, a one-time managing director of Hutchison Whampoa, believes that a great deal of the Li Ka-Shing success formula is fortuitous. He maintains that there never was a grand plan, rather that the great man has used nothing more than 'simple sales techniques'.

Regardless of methodology, Li is now probably the most powerful man in Asia, due largely to his high-level connections in every country in the region, including China itself. Where he scores over so many others is in the widespread nature of his involvements. Were the promises of the mainland economy to bubble up into nothing more than inflation and an unrealisable pipe dream, Li's empire would continue to burgeon elsewhere.

Through his companies, Li is said to be involved in more than HK$1 billion worth of investment in China, but his exposure through additional holdings in Hutchison, Hopewell and other entities makes his real involvement considerably larger, if hard to quantify precisely. The group's direct interest in infrastructure development in China is limited to Shantoo, Li's home town. On the drawing board, however, are plans for three 279.5 MW power plants in Shantao, with a one-third share to be owned by Li's interests; a two-and-a-half-kilometre bridge, again in Shantao, in which Li's party would invest some $670 million; a pier in Liuzhou in Guangxi province; a steel plant in Qinzhou, Guangxi; and two further power plants, in Zhuhai and Hainan.

Cheung Kong creates synergy for the companies it has invested in through business cooperation opportunities, even though it is always a minority shareholder. The company could almost be said to have a formula for printing money, and that formula is based largely on its strategy of reaping profits from booms in property prices, of which Hong Kong has had many. The group is very privileged in being able to invest and trade on a scale that few others can dream of. For example, Cheung Kong's large property bank was used to expand Li's chain of Watson's The Chemist and his Park 'N' Shop grocery stores all over the territory.

Cheung Kong is a traditional, family-run business. The group grew rapidly with the acquisition of Hutchison, and cash flow from property development has fuelled its aggressive expansion to the extent that it is the biggest business empire in Hong Kong and one of the most powerful in Asia. Li remains at the helm, although his elder son Victor has gradually taken over day-to-day operations. Succession will undoubtedly be a seamless progress.

Even the great K. S. Li makes mistakes, something that he is not afraid to admit: he is on record as saying, 'Nobody is God. People are not gods; they are human beings, and human beings make some mistakes. Me too.' His two major forays overseas – with Husky Oil, a petroleum company, and with a Hutchison telecommunications venture, Rabbit – were less than successful. He has made sure, however, that the new Orange telecommunications adventure is learning from Rabbit's mistakes. He is not a man afraid to fail, preferring to take risks in exploration than to never even have tried.

It was through Hutchison that Li unsuccessfully pursued the 35% he did not yet own of the Hong Kong property company, Cavendish International Holdings. Cavendish was set up initially as an offshoot of the Hong Kong Electric group, the sole supplier of electricity to Hong Kong Island and to the islands of Lamma and Ap Lei Chau. Li, who prefers to handle most of the big corporate plays himself, is said to have taken over Hong Kong Electric in just seventeen hours, including his usual eight hours of sleep. The idea was to create a portfolio to contain its non-electric assets, which included the Hong Kong Hilton Hotel, 34% of Hong Kong Electric, 24.5% of Husky Oil of Canada and 50% of International City Holdings, yet another property company. Li did not succeed in this endeavour, even though Cavendish was then chaired by his English right-hand man, Simon Murray. Murray was also managing director of conglomerate Hutchison Whampoa, which encompasses many of Li Ka-Shing's various businesses, ranging from container terminals to telecommunications. At the time, Li was said to be intensely annoyed at his failure to buy Cavendish. He enjoys the momentum and challenge of a deal and does not like to be thwarted. Eventually, however, he did get his way, and the firm is now part of his empire.

Li Ka-Shing's lifestyle is modest for a man of his enormous wealth. He is a competent and keen golfer, which is lucky because many of Hong Kong's deals are done on the course. One associate compared his golf style with his corporate methods, saying that, just as he takes the measure of a company, he is given to sizing up the ball before hitting it. He then takes the shot without further hesitation, just as if it were a company that he has decided to acquire. His visual and commercial acuity is keen. Even his weaknesses are disguised by a strong mask of consummate decision-making ability.

He also spends time playing Chinese chess and cards, and is described by those who take him on as 'a ruthless card player who likes to win'. He is said to employ the same strategy in games as he uses in business: if he loses, he keeps on playing until he wins. He dresses conservatively in classic but not overly expensive clothes, and is said to watch his personal expenditure, even though he has no need ever to worry. He is not without philanthropic tendencies, though, and it is not only to butter up the PRC that he has established a charitable foundation to improve health care and education near Shantou in his native Guangdong.

When people encounter Li in the flesh, they are hardly aware that he is anybody of importance, so low-profile is his demeanour. His physical appearance too is not especially striking: he is slim and bespectacled, and unexceptionally dressed. He is, despite his success, considered a real man of the people. Back at the beginning of the eighties, Li was threatened by a blackmailer with the bombing of a number of Cheung Kong properties. Rather than let the authorities deal with the matter, Li personally met with the miscreant, gave him a suitcase which was partially stuffed with ransom money, and put on such a convincing performance that the man walked straight into the hands of the waiting police. Li's action was both foolhardy and courageous, but he likes to deal with things in his own way, and very much believes, it is said, in his personal fate. Anyone who takes him on should be aware of the force of the man they are up against.

Unlike many taipans with family-owned businesses, it does not look as though Li Ka-Shing will be beset by succession problems. His sons, Victor Li Tzar-kuoi and Richard Li Tzar-kai – in common with many young men of money – do like to zoom around the waters of Hong Kong in a top-of-the-range speedboat. Despite their penchant for toys, however, there is no indication whatsoever that they are in any way less than very serious about one day assuming their father's mantle. Li is said to be thinking of stepping down in the next few years, but few believe he will ever really be strictly hands-off.

The two young men are said to have sat in on numerous business meetings as toddlers, as if to absorb Li Senior's commercial acumen by osmosis. It has reaped rewards, because both are level-headed, serious young men who seem to understand the weight of the corporate tasks they have before them. The chip off the old block is Victor, who looks very much like his father and who, according to the people who know him well, seems to be somewhat similar in temperament. As Cheung Kong's deputy managing director, he has his hands on most of the property portfolio. He also runs the family's Canadian investments. He is a Canadian citizen, and a graduate from Stanford University, with two masters degrees, in engineering and construction management.

Richard, the younger and more outgoing of the two brothers, is deputy chairman of Hutchison Whampoa. Before Hutchison, Richard's baby was Star TV, but that was sold to Rupert Murdoch's News Corporation for about $525 million, a very healthy return on a company that had been nurtured up until that time for only $150m. Richard was educated at a high school in California before going on to Stanford, where he read economics and computer engineering. He also studied for a time at the London Business School. If every family must have a playboy, then Richard would have to fill the role, even though it would be a poor fit. He loves to use the family's million-pound yacht, *Concordia*, and to pilot himself around in top-of-the-range executive jets.

Victor has been happily married since the spring of 1993, and lives at his father's home with his bride. He is said to be anxious to give his father as much support as possible since his mother died. Richard, on the other hand, lives on his own, and maintains that he is far too busy to think about settling down. He is frequently seen around town with some of Hong Kong's most beautiful and eligible young women. Like their father, neither young man is afraid of failure. They both believe that as long as you do your very best and continually work to improve your knowledge and ability, you cannot help but succeed.

As a long-term move, Richard is said to be very committed to developing a career in hi-tech telecommunications, and he may acquire part of a planned Malaysian telecom satellite. For the moment, however, he is deeply involved in life insurance. His father's company, the Pacific Century group, plans to acquire the Singapore company, Seapower Asia Investments. This would give the Lis over 45% of the business which owns Top Glory, one of the fastest-growing insurance companies. The acquisition would also furnish the Li groups with yet another territorial expansion. Top Glory recently hired vast numbers of sales agents out from under its Hong Kong rival, National Mutual, including the latter's Hong Kong chief. They plan to have some 4,000 agents by the end of the decade, which would make them unstoppable in the business.

Robert Kuok, the former 'king of sugar', now in his seventies, is these days concentrating on property development in mainland China and on his plush hotel group, Shangri-la Asia. Like Li

Ka-Shing, he has already been appointed a special adviser to the PRC. His Hong Kong operations started as recently as 1981, with the opening of the Kowloon Shangri-la. The group evolved from the Malaysia-based Kuok group, whose hotel division is operated under the Shangri-la name. All its interests are managed by the privately owned Shangri-la International Hotel Management Ltd. After Kowloon, the company moved into China, with joint ventures in Hangzhou and with the Shangri-la Hotel in Beijing, as well as with 50% ownership of the China World Trade Centre. Other interests include a 39.2% stake in the Beijing Shangri-la Taxi Co. Ltd; the Island Shangri-la Hotel in Hong Kong; the Shangri-la Hotel in Shenzhen, which opened in 1992; a 20% interest in the Shanghai Centre in China; and the Shangri-la International Nanning Hotels.

Kuok is also a major shareholder in SCMP Holdings, the company which owns Hong Kong's leading English-language newspaper, and is therefore one of the region's main pretenders to Rupert Murdoch's throne as supreme newspaper magnate in Asia. Kuok has a 34.9% stake in the company through Kerry Media Ltd, and Malayan United Industrial owns a further 22.15%. The rest is free float in the market. Apart from the daily newspaper, the company is also involved in bookselling and magazine publishing and distribution. Back in 1986, the Hong Kong and Shanghai Banking Corporation and Hutchison Whampoa sold their 34.9% stake in SCMP to Rupert Murdoch's News Corporation. In 1993 Murdoch sold his interest in the company, probably because he believed that the future political complexion of Hong Kong would make life impossible for a foreign-owned newspaper. The question for many today is whether Kuok, with his close commercial kinship to the mainland, will be brave enough to leave the paper as the independent voice that it has always been. There are fears that, owing to both commercial and political pressures, the paper may have to bend with the wind of the most favourable Chinese contracts. No one yet knows.

Although Greater China is very much his commercial stamping ground these days, Kuok is a Malaysian by birth. Like many of the other new taipans, however, he is Chinese by ancestry and has for years owned vast tracts of sugar plantations in the state of Perlis. His sugar trading and refining operations dwarf the business generated specifically by the plantations themselves. He also owns 18% of CITIC Pacific and is probably worth around $1.8 billion. They say that the young Robert showed sharp instincts for business when he was only a toddler in the family grocery store. His big break came trading commodities in the volatile markets of the Second World War.

Kuok's holdings are mostly privately owned. Like nearly all the new taipans', his businesses, particularly his commodities-trading operations, are in the hands of relatives, trusts and offshore companies. It is very common for taipans to set up this sort of structure in their corporate holdings, with the intention of warding off prying eyes and pushing deals that go wrong firmly out of the limelight.

Well up in Kuok's league is the taipan of the New World Development Co. Ltd, Cheng Yu-Tung, who is sixty-nine years old and worth $1.6 billion. Cheng owns the Renaissance and Stouffer hotel chains in the United States, and has recently acquired control of the New York Riverside South apartment project in Manhattan, which used to belong to Donald Trump. His fortune is based on his 40% ownership of NWD Hotels, property and shipping interests.

When he was only fifteen, the young Cheng fled the mainland and the marauding Japanese, ending up in Macau, where he got work, through connections, as an apprentice in a gold shop. Such was his success that he won the hearts of both the owner and his marriageable daughter. Using both advantages, he built up the business so successfully that he became known as 'Hong Kong's King of Jewellery'. Today, as well as his hotel interests, he is also involved in large-scale infrastructural development throughout China, something he has in common with many of the other new taipans.

The structure of Cheng's portfolio is a fairly typical one. He owns 37.25% of NWD Ltd through the company Chow Tai Food Enterprises Ltd. NWD went public only in 1972 but today has a number of internationally located hotels – the New World hotels in Hong Kong, China and throughout South-East Asia. Cheng also owns the newly named Renaissance Hotels Intl Inc., which was born out of his acquisition of The Ramada International chain of hotels and resorts. He also owns 27.5% of Asia Television Ltd, acquired in 1988. Cheng takes a long-term, very committed view towards investment in China, and has 20–25% of the share price of his company allocated to Chinese infrastructure and development projects. Other strings to his complex bow involve construction, engineering, transport, insurance, and telecommunication services. He has embarked on a joint venture, New World Paging, with the Infa Telecom Group to operate paging services in Hong Kong.

Another joint venture, New World Telephone, has secured the licence to provide a fixed telecommunications network service for Hong Kong when Hongkong Telecom's franchise expires.

Another fortune founded on property and hotels is that of H. C. Lee, who together with his family is worth $1.6 billion. They own 50% of Hysan Development, which has control of the Shanghai Commercial Bank and a number of big property developments. H. C., who runs the company, is the grandson of Lee Hysan, the founder of the dynasty. Lee Hysan was reportedly a wholesale distributor of opium in Hong Kong in the 1920s, when the drug was legal and very lucrative as a business. He was also the biggest landlord in Causeway Bay. He was gunned down by an unknown assassin in 1928.

H. C.'s father, Richard, was for many years chairman of the board of directors of the Lee Hysan Estate Co. Ltd. He was educated in Britain, at Queen's College, Oxford, the Hong Kong alumni association of which he ran for a long time. Apart from his British degree, he has law degrees from both the Chinese University and the University of Hong Kong, and was a JP for some years. He is also an OBE and a CBE. He is a softly spoken man who spends most of his time in his penthouse on top of one of Hong Kong's largest luxury housing complexes, Bamboo Grove, where he tends his prized collection of orchids. He and his wife, Esther, have two sons and two daughters.

Gordon Ying-Sheung Wu is the new taipan responsible for building the 302-kilometre Guangzhou-Shenzhen-Zuhai Superhighway. The vital Hong Kong-Guangzhou primary section, which opened in 1994, was made possible by a ten-year joint venture with the PRC. When Wu's company, Hopewell Holdings, was listed in 1972, it specialised in the development of small to medium-sized properties. Since those days it has moved on to major infrastructural projects, including the road scheme, one of the biggest undertakings in Greater China, together with all its attendant peripheral property development. One of the company's main subsidiaries, Consolidated Electric Power Asia Ltd (CEPA), is also engaged in major power projects throughout China and elsewhere in Asia. Together with Li Ka-Shing's Cheung Kong, Hopewell has acquired and is developing a site in Kowloon Bay that will become the HITEC exhibition centre complex.

Not content with the opportunities that Hong Kong and Guangdong could provide, Gordon Wu moved considerably offshore in his involvement with the $3.2 billion development of an integrated rail and road system in Bangkok. In 1991, through his 44.5% ownership of CEPA, he completed the Navotas Power Station in the Philippines. Electricity is to be sold to the Philippine National Power Corporation for a fixed period of twelve years before the ownership of the plant reverts to the Philippines. The crowning glory of Wu's empire is probably his Mega Tower Hotel, a ninety-one-storey commercial and hotel complex that is being built adjacent to the existing Hopewell Centre in Wanchai. It will be one of the tallest buildings in Asia. He has had mixed success with power projects in Indonesia and the Indian sub-continent.

Apart from Kuok, who has come quite recently to the media, the new taipan most involved in movies and showbiz throughout the region is Sir Run Run Shaw. He was also one of the very first of the new taipans. In Hong Kong, he is chairman of three significant media companies, and he holds executive positions in some forty others, both in the territory and abroad. His main involvements are in Shaw Brothers (Hong Kong), primarily focusing these days on the television rather than the cinema industry through its 30.3% stake in TVB; TVE Holdings (in turn 30.3% owned by Shaw Brothers), a diversified entertainment and leisure operation with non-TV business; and Television Broadcasts Ltd, a conglomerate of entertainment and leisure businesses. Sir Run Run, who was born on the mainland in 1907, has two sons and two daughters through his marriage to Lily Mee Chun. He is a slight but highly visible figure in Hong Kong who is often seen at major charity events and is a generous patron.

Founded in 1965, TVB began with the broadcast of both English- and Chinese-language television and went on to establish its own local operations in the United States and the United Kingdom for the direct distribution of home video products. Three years ago the Jade Chinese-language channel was launched in San Francisco, and at the same time the company took the innovative step of bartering for air time on television stations throughout China. Shaw's China play takes him back more or less to where he started over 50 years ago, promoting the Chinese film industry. During the last two years TVB has expanded further on the international scene by entering into an agreement with the Vancouver-based Fairchild Group to acquire Chinese TV stations in Canada. In 1993 a joint venture started in Taiwan to distribute Mandarin-language programmes. The company has also undertaken to provide Chinese-language programming throughout Europe on satellite television.

Dickson Poon is founder and chairman of the luxury-goods retailer, Dickson Concepts, one of the two public companies he controls. Through this vehicle, he holds the retailing and wholesaling rights in Hong Kong and much of Asia to over a dozen of the world's best-known names (Charles Jourdan, Guy Laroche, Ralph Lauren, Hermes, Rolex, Bulgari), as well as manufacturing and selling his own international high-fashion accessories line (S. T. Dupont). He was one of the first to identify and cater to the newly wealthy, status-hungry Hong Kong Chinese and other Asians, with a number of boutiques selling a variety of well-known designer products. Many say that with his eight cars and two boats, his Peak mansion and his beautiful second wife he is Hong Kong's answer to Donald Trump. This comparison, however, ends with the fact that both started out with loans from their father, and both are favourite topics for the media.

The scion of a major Hong Kong watch fortune (his father sold Rolexes), Poon started his serious education at Uppingham, where he acquired his more-English-than-the English habits and demeanour. He then went to Occidental College in Los Angeles, followed by the traditional Chinese period in the family business. Subsequently it was arranged that he should learn as much as he could about luxury retailing by working in the Chopard watch company in Geneva, with whom his father's company had good connections. In 1980, at the age of twenty-three, he returned to Hong Kong and, taking out a loan of HK$5 million from his father, opened up his own watch and jewellery shop in Landmark Place, an extremely prestigious retail area. It was his stated aim at the time to establish a net worth of HK$1 billion (£66 million) before he reached thirty. He succeeded only a few months after that birthday. Today, Poon is worth an estimated HK$1.5 billion (£100 million).

Keeping up with Poon's expansion and growth, not to mention the financing and manoeuvring of his deals, can be something of a challenge for those used to more orthodox processes. He is known to be considering a number of foreign listings for his company, on the Paris Bourse and in London or New York. He claims that his 'internationalisation programme' began as long ago as 1982, when the economy was booming and 1997 was unheard of. However,

131

pressure to move offshore had already begun, because the Sino-British negotiations were starting at that time and there was a widespread preoccupation with mortgage financing for fifteen-year leases. His global expansion can be seen to have started with the acquisition in 1987 of S. T. Dupont. He also started a Thai joint venture in 1988. That same year, two companies were acquired, one at a cost of $260 million to produce and market Guy Laroche watches, pens and lighters, and the second costing $15 million to market Hermes and Chopard watches in Singapore. Also in 1988 he acquired a controlling interest in the Hong Kong Optical Company, later renamed Innovations Holdings, which was sold on to Maxton International in 1994 to raise cash, apparently for further China investment. In 1991, Dickson bought Harvey Nichols for HK$709 million, raising the necessary capital through a rights issue. As of 1992, Harvey Nichols operations were extended to Hong Kong.

In 1992, Poon entered the China market through a joint venture with Jin Jiang, one of Shanghai's largest state-owned enterprises, to develop an upmarket shopping arcade in Shanghai. Another joint venture was with the Yangchang group, a leading state-owned manufacturer with property and hotel investments, to invest in retailing, wholesaling and manufacturing operations in Guangzhou. In 1993 he signed long-term retail/distribution agreements for China with nine leading watch and jewellery companies, including Chopard, Bulgari and Hermes. Also in 1993 he opened a Shenzhen 'lifestyle' store, and his worldwide retail network now stands at 180 outlets.

Although now happily remarried, his early personal life was scarred by the breakdown of his relationship with his first wife, a former dancer and kung fu film actress. He married his second wife, Malaysian beauty queen Michelle Yeo Choo Khueng, in a wedding extravaganza which kept the elite of Hong Kong's business society occupied for two whole days and which filled to the brim both the Regent and the Hilton hotels. To commemorate the occasion, a thousand doves were released at the conclusion of the ceremony, and guests toasted the couple with crystal flown in from Paris especially for the event. Poon has often been accused, somewhat unfairly, of loving the media too much. He is not a media junkie, but rather recognises that in the field of luxury goods, a demand is created by snobbery and the longings of the wannabes. He is not afraid to use any effective tool in business. He has, however, toned down his exposure and can be cagey and somewhat overprepared in interviews these days. In the early years his fresh, uncontrived spontaneity, and his natural charm, made him a pleasure to talk business to. The importance of his position, as well as his increasing maturity, have forced him to quieten down and move towards conservatism.

Apart from the retail industry, Poon has privately also been a principal investor in D&B Films, one of Hong Kong's three largest Cantonese-language film production and distribution companies. Through Dickson Pictures and Entertainment Ltd he promotes pop concerts and owns 20% of all the cinemas in Hong Kong; and through Dickson Music Industries Ltd he has a joint Asian recording venture with EMI.

David Tang is unique among businessmen in Greater China. He would probably like to be considered a taipan, and to many, he probably is. He is on the board of T. T. Tsui's Citybus Ltd, one of Hong Kong's privately owned commuter coach services, which runs The Citybird Express. Each coach provides forty-nine aircraft-style reclining seats, with fold-down trays, breakfast served by hostesses (the Citybirds), television with morning news, lavatories, air conditioning and mobile phones (first thirty seconds free). The coaches provide a deluxe alternative on the one-hour route between Central and Shatin, at an approximate fare of £1.60. Shatin, one of the 'New Towns' in the New Territories, has 2,000 industrial employers and a population of about 510,000, many of whom have to wage a daily battle to get into Hong Kong proper. This kind of brilliant filling of a need, together with Tang's burgeoning cigar empire, based on an exclusive relationship with Havana for the whole of Asia, and, more importantly, his China Club, sited right next to the balcony from which the cadres directed the 1967 riots, no doubt assure him that he *is* a taipan. He is certainly a wheeler-dealer *par excellence*, but his keen sense of humour and desire for public acknowledgement slightly give him away.

In Jardine House, where he has his office, Tang stands out from the rest of the occupants. He is not a 'gweilo', a white man, neither has he ever worked for Jardine Matheson. He is, in fact, the third-generation heir to a local fortune and proprietor of DWC Tang Development Ltd, a small merchant bank. He is actually in a quite extraordinary position. English-educated and a proud Anglophile, yet at the same time a flamboyant Sinophile, he has had both business and personal addresses in London for years, and therefore has no passport worries after 1997. However, he believes that there is a solid future for him in post-colonial Hong Kong: as he has said, 'Here self-interest and flexibility are everything. If you declare your position, you are dead.'

Like Dickson Poon, Tang is not afraid to confront the glare of publicity head on, and he is amiable and intelligent enough to get away with it. His performance on *Whicker's World*, with its cameos of high-life parties and a celebrity existence, must have made many taipans wish the ground would swallow them up. Tang's self-declared motto is MUFTI: Money Up Front Is Terribly Important. 'Beyond that I'm into anything that's not illegal and that makes money,' he has said. His flamboyant dress sense recently started a fashion craze in Hong Kong, involving Chinese pyjamas worn with a button-up jacket.

With his beautiful house with gardens running down to the Saikung waterfront, Tang's lifestyle and bravado make him stand out from the real taipans, who usually shun close or even casual inspection. Tang's main function is as a major facilitator for the taipans, and as such he is immensely influential, one of the most powerful individuals in Hong Kong in terms of connections. He is a businessman himself, of course (what Chinese is not?), but he mostly seems to be used – in the best possible way – as a consummate diplomat, go-between and high-profile front man for those who would prefer to keep their own exposure low-key. In Hong Kong especially, things are not always what they seem.

(ii) GREATER KOREA

Only fifty years ago, Korea was a Japanese colony struggling to survive on its predominantly agrarian economy. Over the last twenty-five years, the country has magnificently re-invented itself through staggering annual growth, averaging more than 8% per annum. It now ranks eleventh among the world's top trading economies, and is the US's eighth largest trading partner. This is in spite of the fact that up until the end of the Cold War, South Korea had to spend as much as 6% of its GNP on national defence to counter a potential invasion from the Communist North. The forty-year-old political battle with its northern neighbour also thwarted South Korea's efforts to trade with Communist countries. Nowadays, however, both conglomerates and smaller Korean companies are making inroads into mainland China, Eastern Europe and the countries of the former Soviet Union.

Korea has become a key global player in the manufacture of cars, electronics, steel and shipbuilding. Many national enterprises are relocating their production bases to countries where they can produce the same goods at the lowest possible cost, in order to cope with increasingly fierce international competition. At the same time, Korean companies are sharpening their global ambitions, with Goldstar, for example, buying a 5% stake in Zenith Electronics in the US, Hyundai cars rolling into Europe, and Samsung involved in oil production in Western Siberia and setting up television plants in Eastern Europe.

Today, the nation stands on the threshold of advanced industrial status as it prepares to join the Organisation for Economic Cooperation and Development. Some say its progress has outpaced even that of its old master, Japan. At the moment it is propelling itself forward with 8.5% GDP growth, making it number two in Asia, just fractionally behind China. Many taipans consider, though, that Korea is still about thirty years behind Japan, and that a great deal of money and effort must now be expended in order to catch up.

Only as recently as 1987 did South Korea start out on the road to real democracy after sixteen years of military rule, with the election by popular vote of its first democratic government, led by President Roh Tae Woo. In 1993, the country inaugurated its first truly civilian head of state in more than three decades. Under the leadership of President Kim Young Sam, the government has embarked on an ambitious programme of economic revitalisation and deregulation. As part of its liberalisation plan, 132 out of 224 business sectors have been newly opened to foreign direct investment, and discussions are underway to open more. The remaining sectors are largely related to mass media, property, financial services and energy.

Kim's plans for the country include projections for per capita GNP to reach $14,000 by 1998. Today, the typical income of an average Korean, despite the country's success as a whole, hovers around $6,500 per annum. Nevertheless, the number of cars on the road has trebled in the last four years alone. The population of some 43.2 million is eager to take further advantage of boosted incomes. They cry out for more and more goods, especially from the United States. With President Kim's new policies designed to relax existing entry barriers and create an atmosphere of fair competition, foreign firms should soon be able to meet Korean consumer demands.

One of the key reasons behind the growth of this country in the last three decades can be found in the solidity of the national business structure. This is made up of a number of diversified business groups, or 'chaebols', which are typically owned by a single family and run by a taipan. One of the taipans, Yoon Young-Suk, president of Daewoo's trading arm, and his chairman, Kim Woo Choong, believe that these big business groups are the very brains of the economy. Competition between families is often cut-throat. There is a mood about the country these days, however, that no longer allows for the traditional tolerance towards the taipans and their chaebols and they increasingly seem to fall into both popular and political disfavour. There is a widespread feeling that family ownership and management represents excessive concentration of power.

The businesses of the five largest Korean conglomerates tend to revolve around financial services, semiconductors, shipbuilding and the textile industry. The ten largest chaebols, however, are diversified into eleven different sectors. This compares with Japan, whose top forty conglomerates operate in only five different sectors. Like the taipans in other countries, these ethnic Korean business leaders grew into their pre-eminent positions of today by establishing an almost unchallengeable presence in a number of different and diversified markets. The linchpin that has historically held all the different subsidiary companies together is consistent rule by the autocrat. No matter how great the diversification, there is always a common thread to tie constituent elements together for speedy and efficient coordination. The taipans of Korea and their business culture are said to be the world's toughest. These businessmen are fearless in their ability to use 'pae-gi', that is, aggressive determination, to overcome obstacles from any quarter.

In Korea, culture is key. Traditionally, the taipans are above all aggressive in business, demanding immediate results. While they can be patient, they tend to want to conclude deals sooner rather than later, whereas a Chinese taipan will often play a waiting game. At the same time, however, the Koreans are well known for holding up transactions until they are sure they understand who they are doing business with and that they will be getting what they are after. Corporate structures and operational organisations are very hierarchical, and in this respect have more in common with the Japanese than the Chinese. The Koreans, though, are less 'country-centric' than the Japanese, and never bother to alter products to make them look as though they have been domestically produced.

In the beginning, the family-dominated businesses all followed a tried-and-trusted route to success by taking advantage of the abundance of cheap workers at home, and borrowing both capital and technical expertise from overseas. The companies were highly geared from the start of operations. For many years, South Korea was intent on following Japan's lead as a mass producer of inexpensive consumer goods, but recently she has found that she has largely been beaten to this by countries such as Mexico and mainland China. The early emphasis on research and development, however, is now thankfully beginning to pay dividends. In the beginning, the chaebols developed imported ideas, streamlining production processes into new and more efficient forms. In 1970, the combined budget for research and development was only 0.39% of GNP. According to government statistics, R&D spending will rise to 5% by the year 2000. In other advanced industrial countries, spending is still budgeted at only 3 to 4%.

To consolidate on their early gains in the world marketplace, the Korean taipans persistently set about improving the education and skills of their workers, to ensure that quality, not just cheaply produced goods, allowed them to maintain their edge. Fearful of losing that competitive advantage, those same taipans are now adopting *en masse* techniques in management and production brought in by legions of American management consultants.

The Korean government's role has been key in the development of all the companies, aiding and abetting corporate growth through its stringent but nevertheless paternalistic industrial, business and educational policies. When the government can no longer tolerate the fierce competition between the various groups, especially in light of what it sees as the benign financial help they are all given, it frequently threatens to merge companies arbitrarily unless they toe the government line. However, Korea's taipans still maintain their hold on the national economy, at least for the time being. To ensure that they remain lean, mean corporate machines, most taipans are now honing their competitiveness by spinning off companies, downsizing and decentralising.

Foreign industrial and commercial advisers were originally hired to boost technical expertise so that domestic manufacturers could develop their own leading edge. A classic example of this can be seen in a Samsung subsidiary, Cheil Wool. To start with, this forty-year-old company relied heavily on imported German and then Japanese skills. It learned so well from its teachers, however, that after just ten years of picking brains and studying machinery, Cheil, alone in Korea at that time, was awarded the prestigious 'all wool' trademark. The company then went on to win international patents for its own technical improvements. Nowadays, Cheil is established as a leading innovator in wool and other textile production, from whom German and Japanese producers often learn a great deal. A more recent example of the successful import of techniques and technology is the Lucky-Goldstar group. In 1991, that company bought a share in Japan's Zenith, so that it could arm itself with the newly developed flat-screen television tube technology, as well as benefit from an infusion of equity and an alliance that would allow it access to plants elsewhere in Asia, in Europe and in the Middle East.

When it comes to education, Singapore is rightly world-renowned for its high standard. Its number of engineers and scientists per head of population nevertheless ranks second to Korea, which today has 22 for every 1,000, compared with Singapore's 5.2 per 1,000. Some 68% of the Koreans who make up the country's workforce graduate from high school, compared with Singapore's 57%.

At the beginning of Korea's industrial growth, wages were low and working conditions arduous. Many employees put in a fifty-six hour week, with perhaps only one day off a month. Women were frequently paid only half as much as their male counterparts. Companies were able to get away with little improvement in the workers' lot for three reasons: there were few opportunities for emigration abroad; the rapid growth in population ensured a labour surplus; and there was an almost complete absence of unions. For two decades, in fact, the Korean Central Intelligence Agency was responsible for all labour policy, and no opposition was brooked from any quarter.

In the late 1980s and the 1990s, however, there has been an increased tendency to labour unrest, bred from years of dissatisfaction, so much so that wages have been forced ever upwards till they have been growing at a rate as high as 20% per annum. Students have been a potent political body, playing a significant role in the industrialisation of Korea along increasingly Western lines by showing solidarity with the country's workers and insisting that the country adopt more complete democracy. When military rule ended in 1987, an explosion of strikes led to the highest wages in Asia outside Japan. The Korean economy is currently experiencing what former president Roh Tae Woo has called 'a grave transition'. However, the strikes of the last eight years or so have in many cases led to the establishment of new labour agreements.

All these factors have contributed significantly to the situation today where Korea's top ten conglomerates account for nearly 70% of the country's GNP. The government has also been responsible for protective import tariffs and quotas, such as those for the car production industry, which have only recently been eased, and for generous public subsidies to promote economic growth. These boosted exports by rewarding a number of 'pet' firms (nearly always those from the chaebol groups) who met the exacting performance requirements.

Many people would justifiably argue that the Korean government has been overly interventionist. For example, more than twenty years ago the car manufacturer, Shinjin, was doubly thwarted by both the oil shock and the innovations that Hyundai had come up with for its Pony car. The company got into financial trouble, at which point the government, rather than lending a helping hand, promptly transferred the Shinjin stock to Daewoo Motors. Similar handling was seen also in the cement industry, when the then largest producer refused to adopt a new production process and found that the ownership of its factories was arbitrarily transferred to another chaebol, that of the Ssangyong Group, who were close to the government.

In terms of finance, Korea's taipans have always depended upon bank loans to fuel their corporate growth and have shown little inclination to dilute their control by selling stock in their companies. Given the scale of their operations in the 1990s, however, it is inevitable that they will need to take their empires further out into the public domain in order to raise the necessary capital. At the moment, many hesitate to go public: only thirteen of Samsung's forty-eight companies, for example, are listed. The taipans will fight every inch of the way to stop power seeping away from them, despite government initiatives to persuade them otherwise.

Korea's stock exchange was opened to foreign investors at the beginning of 1990. The government then introduced monitoring, and a revised Securities and Exchange Law, in an effort to curb share-shuffling and the widespread insider trading that seemed to be occurring, and to prevent some of the greater excesses of a few of the taipans. It has always been notoriously difficult to trace the ownership of the intricately interlinked companies that make up the taipans' domains, largely because of the practice of transferring ownership and wealth to family members through unorthodox stock transactions. Corruption has been a problem in some of the companies, but the large number of salaried and highly professional employees throughout a group's subsidiaries have managed to prevent the chaebols involved from being completely rotten. Until very recently, the taipans were unable to take their wealth out of the country, strictly limited as they were to a $1 million capital transfer limit. Offenders could expect to spend at least ten years in jail, or, if they had really fallen foul, receive a death sentence. All monies earned, therefore, were ploughed back into the family-run corporations.

Korea's government-controlled finance system also played a large part in the success of certain taipans through the regulation of interest rates for the repayment of foreign loans made to Korean companies. By subsidising selected corporate loans, the government could dictate which industries and sectors were pushed and primed for growth and which were held back. They also set strict export targets, and even required that licences be issued to firms wishing to be involved in a particular industrial sector or market, thus regulating the number of companies who could participate. In the last year or so, low-rate state financing has been denied to those chaebols who refuse to fall in line with national policy, which insists that the top ten conglomerates must limit their core business to just three specified sectors, rather than branching out into what are regarded as more speculative areas of expansion.

Korea's financial system was originally nationalised under Japanese colonial rule. Then, forty-five years ago, under Syngman Rhee's presidency, it was privatised at the insistence of the United States Agency for International Development. The US administration also insisted on a programme of widespread land reform, creating a patchwork quilt of small landowners. The military regime that took control of the country in 1961 subsequently nationalised the system again, so that until very recently, the government maintained a tight grip on all financial regulation.

Under President Kim's regime, however, government controls on private-sector business activity are being cut back at all levels. The government says it intends to push ahead with deregulation, internationalisation and economic liberalisation. Financial reforms are gradually being introduced across the board to try to reduce government interference. Furthermore in an attempt to establish 'clean government' and 'economic justice', properties belonging to high-ranking officials and politicians are to be recorded, with the introduction of the real-name financial transaction system. At the same time, the corset of support and regulation that the taipans have found themselves wearing has been considerably loosened. While this may benefit some and impede others, the days of commercial oligarchy are sure to fade. Many of the overprotected and oversegmented business sectors will now find themselves far more exposed to the hazards of a genuine commercial life.

Chung Ju-Young, the taipan of Hyundai, was born a rice farmer's son. His fortune is based on construction, heavy industry and cars, and together with his family he is said to be worth over $2 billion. Hyundai is the largest and most powerful of the Korean car manufacturers, with nearly $9 billion in sales. The group as a whole also includes some of the biggest shipbuilding, steel, cement and paint companies in the world and is the fourth largest conglomerate in South Korea, with forty-two subsidiaries and 22 trillion won (approximately $28 billion) of total assets. Chung and his family own 27.5% of group companies' shares, and subsidiaries own another 40.3%.

In November 1991 Chung Ju-Young became the first highly visible victim in the government's witch-hunting campaign against the excesses of the chaebols. He is said to have made billions of won by buying shares in Hyundai-related companies that were about to be listed on the Korean Stock Exchange. Chung Mong-Ku, one of his sons, made 23.5 billion won in a similar fashion, while a nephew, Chung Mong-Kyu, executive director of Hyundai Motor Services, is said to have engaged in a circuitous device to borrow capital to buy shares, using company money to secure the loan and make the repayments, only then to sell the shares, once listed, at a huge profit and yet still hold more than 27 billion won-worth. The Office of National Tax Administration took several other chaebols to task, including Daelim, Hanjin and Sammi. Chung, together with eight relatives from the Hyundai commercial clan, was ordered to pay some $182 million in back taxes. Amazingly, he declared that not only was he innocent of any wrong-doing, but he was too poor to even consider payment. The government arranged to stop all further credit to Hyundai and to the family's individual members, and took steps to call in outstanding loans that had been made to the company. Chung had no choice but to acquiesce and pay up.

In December 1992, Chung made a rather rash attempt at a presidential bid, perhaps seeing it as the only way to restore the old order that had favoured him and his business empire so strongly. Foolishly, he went on the offensive, accusing the then President Roh of an unwarranted attack on the chaebols. Not prepared to lie down and take his punishment, Chung formed his own party and quickly became an influential political figure, winning 10% of the seats in the parliamentary elections. After this, he relinquished hands-on control of Hyundai's fourteen public companies, a portfolio with an estimated value of $2.6 billion, and in 1993 retired from active management of the company, though he still plays a considerable part in policy-making. The Hyundai group itself suffered substantial financial pressure as a result of Chung's political campaign.

Chung has been succeeded by his younger brother Chung Sei-Young, who is now nominal group chairman as president of Hyundai Motors. Chung the Younger has declared that he will take the group on a less autocratic route, and is quoted as saying that 'Hyundai no longer wants to have the bad image of a chaebol. It will change to an assembly of totally independent companies.' Seven of Chung Senior's sons are now in control of key subsidiaries. Chung Mong-

Kyu, son number two (the eldest was killed in a car crash), has an iron-fist control of the so-called MK Group. Number three son, Chung Mong-Jun, has significant ownership in Hyundai Heavy Industries, and also represents his father's National Party in the national assembly. Related to this family empire is the Keumkang Group, which is 23.9% owned by Chung Senior's youngest brother, Chung Sang-Young. Its two main activities are the Keumkang Corporation, Korea's largest manufacturer of building materials, and Korea Chemicals, the country's largest producer of industrial paints. They naturally do a great deal of business with the Hyundai Corporation. The eldest of the four brothers, Chung In-Young, controls the Halla Group, whose key companies are Hall Cement and the leading car parts manufacturer Mando Machinery.

Chung Ju-Yung made a number of bold moves throughout his somewhat aggressive commercial career, particularly in the establishment of his empire overseas. Hyundai was the first Korean construction company to build bridges in Alaska, housing in Guam and highways in Thailand. There are plans afoot also for car factories in mainland China, most notably in Manchuria, home to more than two million ethnic Koreans.

Like many of his fellow taipans, Chung's concern for quality when his company began operations was low on his list of priorities. However, an increasing number of shipbuilding orders were lost to Hyundai through shoddy production, and the company was forced to pay greater attention to the training of workers and managers in order to achieve higher standards of manufacture. In less than a decade, shipbuilding quality improved so radically that Hyundai started to receive accolades from Lloyd's of London.

Daewoo is one of Korea's biggest companies, headed by taipan Kim Woo-Choong, who is its chairman and founder. Profits for 1993 stood at $580 million, up more than 50% on the previous year. Kim is famous for his nocturnal crawls around the factory floor, looking for flaws, in his search for the ultimate in quality control. Each team of workers in the car assembly plant is led by a quality chief, identified by his luminous green overalls, whose job it is to point out and correct errors.

Fifteen years ago Daewoo entered into a $200 million joint venture with General Motors, and is intensely proud of the results. The partnership is now said to be officially over, the reasons for the split apparently lying in the two companies' differing ambitions: GM wanted a larger role in the Korean market, and to produce a subcompact, the Pontiac LeMans, for the US market; while Kim wanted to take on the world. Having bought out GM's 50% share in Daewoo, at the same time agreeing to manufacture the LeMans for the US, Kim is more determined than ever to beat Japanese competition, despite the fact that his company has favourable ties with both Suzuki (for the production of a mini car for the domestic market) and Isuzu. To this end, Daewoo's workers are regularly sent over to Japan for study programmes to make sure that they are on top of the latest in quality control. At the moment, Daewoo's main buyers come mostly from developing countries. Kim's immediate ambition is to grab a share of the US market, ideally within the next two years. He is also tackling other areas, including the manufacture and export of car components through other joint ventures. One of the leading taipans to attempt to reunite Korea, at least commercially, after the non-aggression pact, Kim Woo-Choong has signed contracts to build factories in North Korea as well.

Daewoo and Kim are flexing their muscles in other sectors too. The closest the country has to a 'celebrity taipan' is Bae Soon Hoon, president of Daewoo Electronics, who appears in TV commercials comparing his company's washing machines and TV sets to reliable, ergonomic and thoroughly useful tanks. The corporation has entered into an agreement for the manufacture of television picture tubes in Vietnam, a move designed to circumvent the spiralling wages in Korea. In Hanoi, skilled workers can be bought for just $50 a month, whereas the same labour in South Korea can be expected to cost $1,500. Kim has also negotiated nine joint venture export factories for clothing and luggage.

Lee Kun-Hee, the taipan of the Samsung electronics giant, with its 180,000 employees, is said to be worth around $1.6 billion. The net group sales of his empire are worth some $49 billion. Samsung's twenty-four companies earned a profit of $600 million last year, up from $376 million the previous year. Amongst the many corporate assets of interest is a half-ownership in a VCR plant in Tianjin in mainland China. Lee is also said to be considering a number of major investments in Vietnam.

Founded by the late Lee Byong-Chull during the Japanese era, the Samsung group has now grown into Korea's largest and most profitable chaebol, and indeed is the largest non-Japanese conglomerate in Asia. It operates companies with controlling local and important international market shares in semiconductors, consumer electronics, food-processing and pharmaceuticals, as well as ship-building, construction, media, electronic components, chemicals, life insurance, non-life insurance, hospitals, hotels and textiles. Lee has also spearheaded activity in retailing and the production of motion pictures. Today, Samsung is the world's biggest producer of DRAM chips, whereas Hyundai, its closest Korean competitor, only just makes the top ten.

Lee Byong-Chull, like Hyundai's founder, had significant problems with the Korean government during his reign as taipan. Lee Kun-Hee, however, appears to enjoy close connections with the Kim administration. Lee Junior, the founder's third son, was at pains for a while after his father's death to keep his distance from the company, the result of a somewhat tortuous father-son relationship. When, almost overnight, he did take over the empire, he did so with total commitment.

Lee has a free hand with Samsung because his eldest brother, Lee Meng-Hee, takes no part whatsoever in the company's daily activities, preferring to concentrate on Cheil Foods & Chemicals which he separated from the group in 1993. This was the first sign that the empire was going to fracture among the family. In turn, Lee Meng-Hee's eldest son, Lee Jae-Hyun, took control. Lee Byong-Chull's widow, Sohn Bok-Nam, controls Samsung Fire & Marine, Korea's leading non-life insurance company, with 12.8% ownership. Her daughter, Lee In-Hee, took control of Hansol Paper, also spinning it off from Samsung, while another daughter, Lee Myung-Hee, holds the reins of the Shinsegae Department Stores, with 20.1% of the shares, and of the Westin Chosun Hotel, which she half owns. The unity of Lee Byong-Chull's single-minded corporate purpose has been dissipated. Samsung under Lee Kun-Hee now wants to concentrate on electronics and chemicals, so the loss of the department store chain and the paper manufacturing business is not considered a problem.

To strengthen Samsung's competitive advantage, Lee Kun-Hee is engaging in a programme of what he terms corporate 'shock therapy'. This therapy last year alone entailed expenditure of more than $1 billion, or 42% of the company's capital budget, on equipment to fine-tune efficiency. Lee has also arranged a campaign of overseas education for his staff, involving visits to retail outlets in the United States, Japan and Germany, where they often have to endure twelve-hour lectures followed by the handing-out of tapes for regular at-home review. His idea is that management should familiarise themselves thoroughly with their market, and also that they should be exposed to the sort of harsh criticism that he knows will be forthcoming from overseas consumers. So committed has Lee been to this commercial revolution that he has vowed that if any of the empire's companies should suffer as a result, the loss will be compensated out of his own pocket. If his policy changes work, on the other hand, he has promised to donate two-thirds of his considerable personal wealth to a foundation for the good of company employees. He declares that he has staked his honour, his life and his assets on his own little corporate *coup d'état*.

Lee has also introduced into his factories the Japanese practice of stopping production lines when problems occur, and he thinks nothing of having as many as 20% of a plant's workers correcting production hitches. He believes that practice makes perfect and that the underscoring of errors makes them less likely to happen again. In a surprise move he has adopted a policy of positive discrimination in the employment of women as managers, and has also limited all workers to a strict eight hours per day, insisting that everyone leave at 4 p.m. Internal meetings, he stipulates, must not last for more than one hour, and internal reports must say what they have to say in just one page. All forms of waste are to be purged. He insists that everyone should 'think global' and concentrate most heavily on boosting trade with mainland China and Russia. Lee believes that rather than just taking orders, everyone should work together to improve production and find solutions. Every meeting of any importance in the company is recorded, with the tape being made freely available to anyone curious enough to want to hear it.

Chey Jong-Hyun, taipan of the Sungkyong group, always perceived his role in life as that of a scholar and semi-ascetic. His father, however, had other ideas, seeing him as the saviour of the family textile business. Today Chey, a master's graduate in both chemistry and economics from the University of Chicago, and his clan are worth at least $1.3 billion. His fortune was considerably boosted when he developed the technology to manufacture synthetic fibres and a number of chemical products. Nowadays the former textile company, of which he owns 25.9%, is a chemical and oil giant. Chey's many other commercial interests include the Sheraton Walker Hill Hotel in Seoul.

As part of his corporate revolution at Sungkyong, Chey established an 'Office of the Chairman for Management and Planning' (OCMP) in New York to brainstorm on behalf of the company's operations. In charge was a senior ex-IBM employee, Ronald D. Olsen, whose remit it was to teach Korean managers to perfect the US operation and to look for new diversification opportunities in Korea and the rest of Asia. Chey's policy of what he terms 'super-excellence' seems to be reaping rewards, with increased production output. Each worker, regardless of rank, is expected to set his personal target to compete with the best available anywhere in the world. All managers are expected to recognise key KFS – Key Factors for Success. Active management participation is highly encouraged at all levels.

The Ssangyong group (not to be confused with the Sungkyong group) was founded by Kim Sung-Kon, who served as a key adviser to the late president Park Chung-Hee and was an important member of the old ruling Republican Party. The group, which is now controlled and managed by his eldest son, Kim Suk-Won, includes Ssangyong Cement, one of Asia's largest cement producers, as well as Ssangyong Oil Refining, a joint venture with Aramco of Saudi Arabia, a key local oil refiner and lubricants producer. They also own Ssangyong Motors, which recently entered into an equity and technology transfer with Mercedes-Benz. Kim Suk-Won is passionate about cars and recently acquired Panther Motors, a loss-making British sports car producer.

Korean Airlines, despite its apparent status as a nationalised airline, is in fact 24.3% owned by taipan Cho Jung-Hoon, who is chairman of the Hanjin group. He started out in business by trucking supplies for the UN forces during the Korean War, and went on to win contracts during the Vietnam War to transport supplies to both American and Korean troops in the field. He manoeuvred successfully to win control of the then loss-making Korean Air airline during the government's privatisation of the company. Cho's interests also encompass holdings in securities and construction, and affiliates include Hanjin Corporation, a major trucking and stevedoring company, and Hanjin Shipping, a leading Korean shipping concern. Among his family, Cho's second son, Cho Su-Ho, manages Hanjin Shipping, while his eldest son, Cho Yang-Ho, runs Hanjin Corporation. Third son Cho Nam-Ho runs the construction concern Hanil Development, which recently won a major contract to build

Korea's new international airport. Youngest son Cho Chung-Ho manages Hanjin Investment and Finance.

Construction taipan Choi Wonsuk controls the Dong Ah group as son of its founder, the late Choi Jun-Mun. The group does not include many affiliates, but does feature companies with an important presence in their respective industries. Dong Ah Construction, of which Choi owns 10.1%, is one of Korea's leading public works contractors and a major overseas builder. Korea Express, in which he also has a 10.1% stake, is the country's leading trucking concern. He also owns 13.9% of Kongyung Construction. Choi is involved in stockbroking, too, through his 11.9% stake in Dong Ah Securities. Unlike many other Korean chaebols, Dong Ah companies do not feature extensive cross-holdings. The chairman has individual stakes directly in each company. Choi's elder sister, Choi Eun-Jung, controls Dong Ah Life Insurance.

Kim Seung-Yon is the son of the late Kim Jong-Hee, founder of another leading Korean conglomerate, the Hanwha group. Although Kim Seung-Yon, the eldest son, manages the group's key companies, there has been considerable family squabbling over, among other things, their ice cream producer, Bingrae, and the group's retailing operations, Hangyang Stores. Second son Kim Ho-Yon is currently in charge of these, but there is still internecine warfare involving Kim Jong-Hee's only daughter, Kim Young-Hye, over the control of First Fire and Marine Insurance. As a whole, Hanwha's main focus lies in the chemical sector and in military ordnance supplies. Hanwha Corporation was previously known as the Korea Explosives Corporation and is the country's only supplier of military equipment and arms. The group also controls major holdings in Hanyan Chemical – producers of ethylene, PVC resins and PVC-based building materials – and in the major petroleum refiner Kyungin Energy.

The Lotte group is a company well known to anyone who has spent time in Japan. Lotte's taipan, whose fortune is multiplying on a commercial empire of department stores and confectionery, is Shin Kyuk-ho. Worth over $6 billion, he is thought to be Korea's richest man. At the age of twenty-one, he moved to Japan, where he founded his fortune on chewing gum. He then expanded into property and established his Lotte group of stores, in both Korea and Japan. The secret of his success lies in a canny talent for promotion. His family between them own 41.4% of the Lotte group, which also has interests in hotels.

The Ku and Huh families still control all the companies of the Lucky-Goldstar group, which was started by two men from the same village in Korea's South Kyongsang province. They began by producing face creams, and then moved on to the manufacture of combs and toothbrushes. Later on, diversification led the company into televisions, refrigerators and other consumer electronics. Nowadays, the Goldstar side of the group specialises in electronics, whilst the Lucky side revolves around chemicals. The current chairman, Ku Ja-Kyong, the eldest son of founder Ku In-Hoi, sticks firmly to the Confucian tradition of family loyalty and believes in harmony among men. Strangely enough, extensive cross-holdings exist within each half of the group but very few between them. The relationship between the two entities is characterised by the twin towers of their corporate headquarters. The group is controlled by family members, who serve in senior positions in each affiliate. Lucky-Goldstar is somewhat unusual in that it has survived intact the death of its founder.

The late Lee Yang-Ku, who founded the Tongyang group, had no sons to succeed him. His daughters, however, Lee Hyekyung and Lee Hwakyung, are both involved in the family business. The former's husband, Hyun Jaehyun, is chairman of Tongyang Cement, the larger of the two original companies and the entity with the most extensive control of group affiliates. It is nevertheless his wife, one of the very few truly powerful female taipans in Korea, who personally owns and controls the largest block of shares in the company. Through an affiliate, Tongyang Investment & Finance, this side of the family has gained control of data and international telecommunications in Korea. Lee's other daughter, Lee Hwa-kyung, controls Tongyang Confectionery.

The 'hat king' of Korea, Sung-Hak Baik, who was born in Manchuria but moved with his mother to North Korea when he was five years old, is today the world's largest hat manufacturer. He is said to have a net worth of $300 million and is one of Korea's largest individual landowners. He began his solely owned Young An Hat company over thirty-five years ago, and today produces sixty million hats a year, mostly baseball caps under licence from the American major leagues. Baik supplies 20% of the American market of 180 million hats a year, and 40% of the world licensed market of sixty million caps. He has sales in forty countries and revenue of approximately $150 million a year from manufacturing and wholesaling. Further income of about $50 million a year comes from his other businesses, which include textiles and plastics, hotels, supermarkets and farming.

In 1950, at the age of ten, Baik was peddling sweets on a boat when it set sail and he found himself – by accident, he says – in South Korea. He took this as a sign that he was meant to move on and settled in the south, even though it meant that he never saw his mother or any of his other relatives in the north again.

Once in the south, he stumbled across Hongchon, a US military base north of Seoul, and there met the family of David Beattie, a member of the US military stationed in Korea, who took the small boy and brought him up. Baik joined a hat company as a janitor, but soon moved on to the production line, where he learned his craft. He then went into the retail side before starting his own business, just nine years after leaving North Korea. The company really took off in 1961 when, after President Syngman Rhee was overthrown in a coup, the government banned the import of many goods, including hats. Sales soared and Baik started exporting hats to Japan and importing from the United States. It was from his American associates, particularly his 'Jewish godfather', Abe Yeddis, that Baik says he really learned his trade.

Baik, who spends half of each year travelling, owns six factories in Korea, as well as manufacturing operations in Arizona, Oklahoma, Texas, Canada, Bangladesh, China and Sri Lanka. He also owns vast tracts of Cheju Island, where he is building a tourist resort. He is a Presbyterian, who donates between 10 and 30% of each year's profits to charity, and has set up a number of scholarship funds for students. Twelve years ago, he also established an orphanage and medical centre known as Baik's Village on a fifty-acre plot of land that used to be the military base where he was rescued by Beattie.

(iii) EAST ASIA – INDONESIA, THE PHILIPPINES AND THAILAND

Indonesia is the fourth largest country in the world. It is made up of 13,677 equatorial islands which stretch over an area the same size as the United States. It is also the largest Muslim country in the world, though there is very little applied fundamentalism, let alone fanaticism. Most of Indonesia's 182 million people live on Java, whose capital is Jakarta, the biggest city in South-East Asia, although Sumatra and Bali are also well populated. Half of the population are under thirty years old, and less than 1% of Indonesians have any sort of post-secondary education.

Even in these most unlikely of conditions, there are taipans. Many are involved in selling products to the government through a 'pet' local agent who knows no business style except pure corruption. They may not like the system, but it is the only one available. Certainly in the last few years, Indonesia has been taking something of a free market route, but there are still large numbers of state enterprises that are shored up by the government despite staggering inefficiency. Nevertheless, Jakarta, Batam and even Bali are all working hard to increase their industrial bases, with modern factories, office buildings and shopping centres becoming common sights.

The labour force grows by 2.5 million people each year, all working for wages lower than those in Guangdong province. Despite this, there is a definable and growing middle class. Indonesian textile workers make only $2.50 a day, about 10% of what South Koreans get and well below the $4 daily wage in booming South China. This inexpensive labour surplus is extremely desirable in the Asian-Pacific Rim, where so many countries are facing a labour shortage. Indonesia is the world's largest exporter of liquefied natural gas, the biggest tin producer, and a major supplier of wood products. By making use of these human and natural resources, the standard of living in Indonesia is anticipated to reach, by the year 2000, a per capita income of $1,000 per annum. The economy has grown since 1967 alone at an average rate of 7% a year, and is among the ten fastest growing in the world, according to the World Bank. Per capita income has already increased from $50 a year to around $730, around half that of Thailand. Recently, the first Islamic bank opened for business in Jakarta.

Jakarta, with its 8.2 million inhabitants, has grown up remarkably quickly in the last decade, so much so that its skyscrapers and office blocks now look much like those in Hong Kong or Singapore. The main difference is that, with a relatively new infrastructure power failures occur in both electricity and telecommunications, making global business dealings something of a daily nightmare. Other complications include relentless palm-greasing problems, an unwieldy bureaucracy, and 'guanxi' which are even more tightly knit and strictly adhered to than in the most orthodox of Confucian societies. Carefully nurtured business friendships are the only way to succeed in commerce.

Though not truly taipans, there is a powerful faction of business people – who all happen to be members of President Suharto's family – to whom due deference has to be given in any major business deal. Even mighty AT&T and General Motors were forced into ventures with various members of the Suharto clan as a prerequisite to doing any sort of business there at all. AT&T Network Systems was given a $100 million contract, after President Bush's personal appeal to Suharto, to assemble digital switching systems. One of the preconditions was that the company was required to invest $25 million in a new plant near Jakarta and to set up a joint venture with Citra Telekomunikasi, a local and recent addition to the telecommunications industry. Citra is controlled by Mrs Siti Hardijantia, daughter of President Suharto's wife, Rukmana. Indonesia has functioned this way for many years.

Unsurprisingly, the biggest taipan in Indonesia is 'Bapak' ('Big Daddy') Suharto himself. Now aged seventy-three, he has ruled the political roost for twenty-five years. Together with his 'Berkeley mafia' of California-educated advisers, who call themselves 'technologists', Suharto set about encouraging a programme of foreign investment, ideally around the $10 billion a year mark, to be focused on his country rather than mainland China, with whom there is keen competition. This became especially urgent after the collapse of the oil economy in the mid 1980s. Indonesia is the only Asian member of OPEC, but in 1991 oil accounted for no more than one-third of exports, down from 82% in 1981. This programme of 'deregulation and debureaucratisation' has allowed the country to move from its dependency on energy sales, which have fallen from 56% of export revenue in 1986 to only 31% today.

More recently, President Suharto threw out some of his free-market advisers in favour of men like family friend B. J. Habibie, a

German-educated engineer who favours state-run enterprises. As Minister of Research and Technology, Habibie has embarked on a high-tech mission in which, amongst other ventures, he has arranged for investment of $1 billion in a state-owned aircraft factory. This could have something to do with the fact that he worked for many years as a senior researcher for Messerschmitt in Germany, before coming home and persuading President Suharto to bankroll an Indonesian aircraft factory in Bandung. He has also formed a joint venture with General Electric and bought $12 million worth of German ships to be modernised in a state-owned Indonesian shipyard at a cost of over $1 billion. Furthermore, he was instrumental in arranging for Indonesia to buy twenty-four Hawker fighter planes from British Aerospace.

Despite the fact that overseas companies tend to be more than a little put off by the requirement that each new venture must have a letter of approval from Suharto himself, a number of major Japanese, Korean, Taiwanese and even American companies have persisted, and are now taking advantage of the cheap labour to establish offshore production centres in the country. A recent influx of investors, particularly from Taiwan, has given Surabaja, in eastern Java, the highest economic growth rate in South-East Asia. This push for foreign investment is seen as the only solution to Indonesia's debt problem, which amounts to around $10 billion, equivalent to the total assets of all the state banks. Lending money in Indonesia is too often a question of relationships rather than of genuine credit-worthiness. Debt, at the moment, eats away at 30% of export earnings. It is only the World Bank and countries like Japan, with aid worth around $5.5 billion a year, which have saved Indonesia from breaking its own financial neck.

Given the precariousness of both the commercial and the political situation, Indonesia's new taipans wisely keep the lowest of profiles. They are predominantly ethnic Chinese, although the racial group in its entirety constitutes less than 2% of Indonesia's population. Chinese-language newspapers and schools were outlawed a long time ago, forcing most ethnic Chinese to assimilate as best they could into the local culture. One of these new taipans is Prajogo Pangestu (Chinese name, Phang Djun Phen), chairman of Barito Pacific Timber, the largest national private business group in the plywood and related sector. Born in western Kalimantan, where he spent several years as a minibus conductor, Prajogo now owns 10%

of PT Astra International, and concessions for forestry amounting to some 7.14 million acres, and is among the largest plywood producers on earth. In mainland China, he has taken part in the construction of toll roads and manufacturing plants.

The best-known Indonesian on the world stage is Soedono Salim (or Liem Sioe Liong), who is the head of the family-run Salim group, with about $9 billion in annual sales. In the 1940s Liem, who is said to be worth around $3 billion, was a trader who supplied the freedom fighters of Indonesia. The company was started forty years ago and is today the biggest national business group in the country. It is also one of the most powerful conglomerates in the Asian-Pacific Rim, with interests in the US, Europe, Australia, New Zealand and throughout Asia. The core businesses are in cement manufacturing, flour-milling, edible oils, automotive manufacturing, chemicals, property development, banking, leasing and insurance. The Salims own 40% of First Pacific Investment, whose subsidiary, First Pacific Company, is a powerful force in Hong Kong in property and banking.

Salim also, of course, has powerful political connections, having taken care to cultivate Suharto's friendship. In the 1950s, when the President was only a regional commander in central Java, he was desperate for food for his troops, and Liem stepped in to feed the men. His reward was a number of quasi-monopolies, for flour (Bogasari Flour) and cement (Indocement). Now he is also a global player in petrochemicals, plantations and consumer goods, the largest noodle-maker on earth, and the local distributor for Volvo. He controls banks in Indonesia, Hong Kong, and California, and owns Singapore's UIC property giant. A significant China player these days, Liem plans to invest around $1 billion in projects in Fujian, his ancestral province.

Another taipan close to Suharto is Rachman Halim (or Tjoa To Hing), whose family origins also lie in Fujian province. Rachman made his fortune from Indonesia's largest clove cigarette manufacturer, Gudang Garam. The family also own a bank.

In the mid seventies, taipan Mochtar Riady set up the Lippo group, one of the most powerful Indonesian conglomerates. Today, the family's business, with $6 billion worth of assets, lies in finance (they own the oldest overseas Chinese bank in the United States, now called the Lippo Bank California), investment, property, banking and the manufacture of electrical appliances and components, automotive parts and clothing. Mochtar Riady was given a major kick-start by Liem Sioe Liong, who hired him to run the Bank of Central Asia in return for a portion of the equity. For this reason, ties with Soedono Salim's group are very close. Mochtar's sons, James and Andrew, help their father on a day-to-day basis in the management of Lippo, while their brother Stephen runs the Hong Kong operations of the group. He helped to set up several Hong Kong public companies for Lippo, which together are capitalised at nearly $3 billion. Li Ka-Shing, of Hong Kong's Cheung Kong and Hutchison, has taken a 9.4% stake in Riady's group.

The biggest private business in Indonesia in the manufacture of both pulp and paper and edible oils is the Sinar Mas group, the country's second largest conglomerate, with $2 billion in sales. It was established by taipan Eka Tijpta Widjaja (or Oei Ek Tjong) over thirty years ago. Born a Fujian shopkeeper's son, he spent the early part of his life as a copra trader. He is now thought to be worth around $2.7 billion. During the last thirteen years, the group has diversified into banking and financial services, and they are also expanding into leasing, insurance, shipping and printing. Widjaja, who has a fondness for wearing diamond-studded belts, is keen to boost the companies' activities all around the world, and relentlessly borrows money for that purpose. Keen to honour his Chinese heritage, he is making a number of investments on the mainland, including a $34 million pulp and paper plant.

Ferry Teguh Sentosa and his family began the Ometraco group over thirty years ago for the distribution and sole agency of technical goods and industrial machinery. They later moved on to property management and the export of animal feed, and also own 66.19% of PT Bank Tiara. Also interesting are the business operations of Suhargo Gondokusumo and his sons, which date back over forty years and today make up the Dharmala group, with a number of different interests in agro-industry, plastics, finance, insurance, commercial property and housing development.

One of the best regarded of the taipan empires is the H.M. Sampoerna Company run by the Sampoerna family – the country's leading makers of the highly successful handrolled 'Kretek' cigarettes.

The Gajah Tunggal group was established by the Nursalim family, led by taipan Sjamsul Nursalim, in the early 1950s, and today continues with tube, tyre, paint and telephone cable manufacturing, as well as activities in the insurance, financial and banking sectors. The

Bakrie brothers, Achmad and Aboejamin, set up the Bakrie group over forty years ago for the distribution and export of agriculturally related products such as rubber, pepper and coffee beans. They diversified after a few years into the manufacture of steel pipes and rubber gloves, and then on, as is so often the case, into banking, with the PDFCI Bank, in which the family holds a 0.9% share. The company is now largely run by Achmad's eldest son, Aburizal, but all the family work together in day-to-day management. Finally, there is Sofjan Wanandi, who is the chairman of the Gemala group, manufacturers of auto components and pharmaceuticals. The family-controlled company, with $1.5 billion in annual sales, has been buying into Western businesses with brand names and distribution facilities, including Trailmobile, a maker of truck trailers, and battery manufacturers in Britain and Australia.

Also lying in East Asia are the Philippines where, despite the country's proximity to Indonesia, the taipans find themselves playing by an altogether different set of rules. There is nevertheless a continued flavour of individual ties and loyalties and strong family connections. Under Marcos, the business network of mutual back-scratching was not dissimilar to that seen in Indonesia. Since his demise, however, there have been genuine efforts to liberalise both laws and policies for foreign investment in order to stimulate the economy and transform and modernise the country's business structure. The taipans, though, have largely remained the same. Circumstances have been difficult for years, so change of any kind is merely another challenge and does not necessarily cause problems. On the contrary, for many it has opened new avenues down which money can be made.

A newly influential group of taipans in the Philippines, the most powerful of whom are increasingly Filipino-Chinese, is that made up of thirty-something MBA graduates from British, American and Australian universities. They have burst back on the domestic scene in a frantic rush to implement newly learned ideas in their family-owned operations. Their ascendancy is something of an unexpected challenge to the long-dominant Spanish mestizo groups such as the Sorianos and the Ayalas. While the latter families continue to dominate the stock market and manage their businesses professionally, it is in the banking sector that the young returnees are making the biggest impact. For the first time, twenty-five of the country's largest banks are being run by executives who are not major shareholders.

The seeds of this new Chinese business ascendancy in the Philippines, where the group make up only 1% of the population, date back to the mid 1970s, when the country's naturalisation laws were liberalised and President Marcos re-established diplomatic relations with the People's Republic of China. In the 1990s, Chinese-Filipino interests control a number of sectors apart from banking, including commerce, newspaper publishing, property, retailing, textiles, and food and cigarette manufacturing.

The Soriano family, headed by Andres Soriano III, used to own the beer brewing company, San Miguel, but now hold only a 1% stake in the San Miguel conglomerate, which has diversified into investment, container handling, and mining. They also own more than forty different companies. One subsidiary in which they have a quarter share is Anscor, through which they own 15% of Asian Bank, 40% of Seven Seas Resort and various insurance, capital, aviation, steamship, travel and printing assets. Andres runs the family business with his brothers, Carlos and Eduardo, both graduates of the University of Pennsylvania.

Jaime Zobel de Ayala and his family own 67% of the largely debt-free Ayala Corporation, the largest and most diversified conglomerate in the Philippines, with interests in property, food manufacturing, agribusiness, electronics, information technology, insurance and financial services. 'Don' Jaime has a personal net worth estimated at $1.2 billion. He is a Harvard graduate in architecture, and sits on the boards of a number of Western multinationals, including Shell and IBM in the Philippines. His heir apparent is his eldest son, Jaime August Zobel de Ayala II, also a graduate of Harvard. A younger son, Fernando, is a director of Ayala Land Inc. and a number of other subsidiaries, and is in charge on a daily basis of the group's commercial centres.

Other key companies run by the family include Cebu Holdings Inc. (the Cebu Business Park) and Ayala Hotels Inc. – a joint venture with Robert Kuok. With Globe Telecom and Ayala Systems Technology Inc., the clan have also embarked on projects in electronics and telecommunications, neither of which for the moment looks overly promising. They own most of Ayala Land Inc. and half of Ayala Hotels, as well as 41% of the Bank of the Philippine Islands. Ten years ago, the group started seriously looking to expand overseas, with the establishment of AYC Overseas Ltd.

The second oldest of the Filipino taipans' operations is that of the former ambassador to the PRC under Aquino, Alfonso Yuchengco. The family business, the Malayan group, has interests in insurance, finance, telecommunications, gold mining, oil exploration, construction, hotels and banking. Sixty-five years ago, Alfonso's father, Enrique, founded China Insurance, which subsequently became known as the Malayan Insurance Co. Nowadays, the family concentrates more on telecommunications, through their 77% ownership of the Philippine Telecom Investment Company. It is Helen Yuchengco-Dee, Alfonso's daughter, who is generally acknowledged to be the heir to operations. She is currently President of Pan Malayan Investment.

The Cojuangcos, originally Chinese immigrants to the rice and sugar plantations, are one of the best known families in the Philippines. They are heavily involved in sugar, telecommunications, aviation and manufacturing of various kinds. They hold key shares in the Bank of Commerce, Landmark Corporation, Philippine Airlines, and the Manila Chronicle Publishing Company. The taipan, Antonio, or 'Tony Boy', is the nephew of Eduardo Cojuangco, a well-known associate of Ferdinand Marcos. He is also a nephew of former president Corazon Aquino. His father was Ramon Cojuangco, the founder of the Philippine Long Distance Telephone Company, in which the family retains a 10.4% stake. The Cojuangcos, like the Ayalas, are involved with Robert Kuok's Philippine business operations, and Antonio is a director on Kuok's local board. With the Cheng family, the Cojuangcos run The Landmark, a highly successful department store in the Philippines.

John Gokongwei Jr (or Go Kong Wei) is a native of Fukien province in China. The family's fortune was wiped out in the Second World War, and John built it up again, starting with a corn starch factory. Now he is worth $1.1 billion. Together with his son Lance, daughter Robina, and other relatives, he owns 73% of J. G. Summit Holdings, which was originally composed out of his mother's textile company and a number of small snack-food companies, including Universal Corn Products. One of the family's first property projects was the Manila Midtown Hotel in Ermita, which they developed twenty years ago. Today their operations include unlisted companies in textiles and foods, power generation and telecommunications. Robina runs the *Manila Times*, a daily paper, and is in charge of the family department store operations. Their main listed corporate activities include interests in Robinson's Land, URC, CFC/Robina (food), PCI Bank (with the Lopez family), Oriental Petroleum and Far East Bank. One of John's brothers, Henry, runs the food business, another, Johnson Robert, the agribusiness, sugar milling and hotels, and a third, James, controls the consumer goods division. A fourth brother, Ignacio, looks after the family business in Cebu.

The Lopez family, scions of Benpres Holdings and major land-owners since the turn of the century, were very close indeed to former Philippine president Ferdinand Marcos. Eugenio M. Lopez Jr, a masters graduate of Harvard Business School, was at one time vice president. Such proximity, however, did not protect their for-tune when Marcos turned against them, nationalised most of their business and sent them running out of the country. The Lopez money came originally from sugar plantations but metamorphosed into energy, mass media, shipping and banking. The family returned from their exile in 1986, when Corazon Aquino became president. Now Oscar Lopez, Eugenio's brother, runs First Philippine Hold-ings; Eugenio's son, Gabby, runs ABS-CBN (communications satel-lite, telex and telephone operations and cable TV); and his youngest brother, Manuel, is president of Meralco, which owns 40% of the energy company First Private Power Corporation.

Henry Sy (or Si Tsi Xing) is a self-made multimillionaire who owns Shoemart and a significant number of shopping malls. He emigrated at the age of twelve from Long Hu Hong Xi in Fujian province, where he was born, and opened his first shoe shop in Manila nearly fifty years ago, after buying shoes from American servicemen. He is also involved in the SM shopping megamalls (through his company SM Investments); in the Banco di Oro finan-cial institution; in Fortune Cement; and in ship repair (through a 60% owned subsidiary, SM-Keppel Straits Land). The Sys are in partnership with Straits Steamship Land of Singapore to develop a four-billion-pesos property complex, and were also behind the development of the Rit Towers in Metro Manila's Makati district. In mainland China, Sy owns the Xiamen Hotel, and is building more of his megamalls.

Sy has four sons, Henry Jr, Herbert, Hans and Harley. Henry Jr runs the Keppel Philippine Holdings company, Herbert the super-markets and car accessories division, and Hans group operations and engineering. Harley is in charge of merchandising. There is also a daughter, Teresita Sy-Coson, who runs Shoemart Inc. as president, and also the Banco de Oro Savings and Mortgage Bank.

The Concepcion group's core business was originally flour-milling, but its modern-day flagship, the RFM (Republic Flour Mills) Corporation, is one of the biggest food corporations in the country, with activities also in the dairy and bottling industries, and is ranked second only to the San Miguel Corporation in the stock market. Jose N. Concepcion, the current taipan, is helped in the management of the business by a daughter, Eumelia, and three sons, Raul, Jose Jr, and Reynaldo. The family is related to the Araneta clan. Like the Cojuangcos, the Concepcions have a strong link with Indonesia, through a joint venture with Salim's PT Indofood for the production of ice cream and instant noodles.

Lucio Tan (or Tan Ing Chai) began his commercial life with his Himmel corn starch, and is now said to be worth $1.8 billion. As a boy, he supported his family by cleaning out factories, but now controls some of his country's biggest, including the giant Philippine Enterprises, Asia Brewery, and Fortune Tobacco. He also owns the Allied Bank, Foremost Farms, a slew of hotels and a chunk of Philippine Airlines.

Other Filipino taipans worthy of mention are the Ramos family, headed by Alfredo 'Fred' Ramos, who controls the Philodrill Corporation, an oil exploration company. Together with the Kuok group, the company has a joint venture with a 39% stake in Shangri-la Properties Inc. The group also owns the Philippines' largest chain of bookshops, National Bookstore, which is the local licensee of the Hallmark card company, and of publishers McGraw-Hill, and Prentice Hall. Ramos associate Henry Brimo and his son and heir Gerardo together run the Brimo group, which grew out of the family textile business but is now one of the foremost mining companies in the country, through the Philex Mining Corporation. Also notable is Roberto Coyiuto of the Coyiuto group, a key figure in stockbroking and insurance.

Thailand is a territory with its own business rules and tactics that have nothing in common with either Indonesia or the Philippines. The concept of nation, religion and monarchy is the bedrock of Thai society and of the Thai cultural heritage. The waves of migration from south-west China are thought to have started as early as the seventh century, and there are now significant numbers of ethnic Chinese in the country and amongst the taipans there. The turbulence of Thai politics, with frequent changes in prime minister, numerous elections, and near civil war, seems miraculously to leave business largely untroubled. Such is the strength of local entrepreneurial fervour that the annual growth rates for the country as a whole usually hover around 8% per annum, putting Western countries to shame. The GDP has gone from $775 to $1,420 per person in a period of just four years, and shows signs of increasing still further.

The country's most visible taipan, said to be worth well over $2 billion, is Dhanin Chearavanont (or Chia Kok Min), who controls the C. P. Pokhphand group. The Chearavanont family owns just over 70% of the stockholding of the group, but its other unlisted assets are impossible to quantify in the mysteries of the Bangkok financial world. The group itself, though, has more than 200 companies (ten of them listed on various South-East Asian stock exchanges) and sales of around $4 billion a year. C. P. Pokhphand is in league with America's Wal-Mart to open retail outlets in mainland China and Hong Kong. Dhanin was the youngest of four sons born to Chinese parents who emigrated to Thailand in 1919. His father and uncle, Chia Ek Chaw and Chia Seow Whooy, arrived in Bangkok from southern China to sell seed and fertiliser. From those small beginnings, the company has grown to become one of the world's biggest producers of animal feed, employing 24,000 people.

At the age of twenty-five, Dhanin assumed control of his father's feedstuff business. He specialised in increasing yield by copying US farming production methods, which he pioneered in Asia. During the life of the company, Thailand's consumption of poultry has coincidentally risen tenfold to 22lb a year per person. C. P. has been so successful that the company has branched out into owning the local 7-11 franchise, a chain of Chester's sit-down grilled chicken restaurants, and a network of 300 company-operated 5-Star Brand carry-out chicken shops.

In the early 1970s, C. P. expanded into Indonesia, Singapore, Malaysia, Taiwan and Hong Kong, and more recently into Turkey and Portugal. More than 60% of the group's income originates in mainland China. C. P. is the joint venture partner of Kentucky Fried Chicken in Bangkok and Shanghai, and supplies chicken to KFC in Beijing, Hong Kong and Singapore. In the Japanese market, Thailand, thanks to Dhanin's efforts, has in the last few years edged out the US as the leading supplier of chicken. Every possible use for by-products in the business is considered. One recent spin-off is crocodile farms, where the reptiles are harvested for meat and hides, and are fed, of course, on chicken scraps.

Chearavanont has recently also started to diversify heavily into petrochemicals: he is involved in a $320 million PVC joint venture with Belgium's Solvay. In China, he is in partnership with Honda, producing 200,000 motorcycles a year. Together with Siemens and New York telephone company Nynex Inc., the C. P. group is also investing $3 billion in a two-million-line telephone concession in Bangkok. Other joint ventures include relationships with Holland's Makro for retailing, Japan's Seiyu for supermarkets and Mitsubishi for prawn culture, and beer with Heineken. Five years ago, the group teamed up with British Telecom to win Thailand's biggest-ever infrastructure contract. Those who know Dhanin well say that it was clear from the beginning that chicken feed was not going to be a big enough venture to contain him. He himself attributes his success only to his good luck in being in the right business at the right time in the right place. His hobbies are appropriate for a chicken farmer: he breeds and races homing pigeons, and also breeds Thai fighting cocks.

Another major Thai taipan, and one who is relatively new on the scene, is Thaksin Shinawatra, a fourth-generation Thai whose family originally came from Taechew in China. His grandfather started what became one of the country's largest silk-producing companies, and his father was a prominent politician. Thaksin trained to be a police officer, but today figures large in the growing world-wide cellular communications industry. He is chairman of Shinawatra Computer & Communications Co., one of the sector's fastest-growing regional companies. The group has concessions in cellular telephones, radio-paging, subscription television, data communications, telephone directories and satellite communications that currently earn them sales of $400 million a year.

A doctoral graduate in criminal justice from Sam Houston State University in Huntsville, Texas, Shinawatra began by buying IBM computers for US dollars and leasing them to the Thai government for the Thai currency, the baht, thus benefiting from the exchange rate. He then signed a build-transfer-operate (BTO) contract with the government, and in the process acquired part ownership of a local cellular communications network, Advanced Info Service. Cellular was the only way to break into the communications business. In a country where it can take four years to get a telephone from the government's telecommunications monopoly, it is easy to see why Shinawatra's enterprise is paying such huge dividends. The company currently enjoys profits of around $35 million a year, with large year-on-year increases.

In the early days, Thaksin's wife, Potjaman, ran the business while he kept his regular job in the police force, where he stayed till as recently as 1987. By that time Shinawatra had 120 employees and was making $300,000 a year from distributing both IBM and AT& T's products. In 1990, the company succeeded in getting its twenty-year cellular licence, paying around $530 million to outbid the opposition. In return, Shinawatra gets concession payments of 15% of total sales for the first five years, rising 5% each five years to 30% of revenues for the last five years. A cash cow for the future.

Four years ago, Thaksin took an important step in expanding his cellular and TV services into Asia, especially into neighbouring Indochina (Vietnam, Cambodia and Laos), by winning a thirty-year government concession to operate Shinawatra Satellite, with twelve-transponder satellites built by Hughes Aircraft and launched by Arianespace. As part of the scheme of things, Shinawatra Computer & Communications also has a 55% stake in International Broadcast Corporation, with five broadcast channels, including CNN, and more than 100,000 subscribers to date.

The Sophonpanich family are one of Thailand's wealthiest and most influential business clans, thought to be worth around $1.5 billion. Their fortune comes largely from their 25% ownership of Bangkok Bank – one of the hottest overseas stocks for Americans and other foreign investors buying in the Thai stock market – which today has branches all over the world, including Beijing, Shanghai and Shantou. It was the late Chin Sophonpanich who made the bank the force it is today. In 1988, he was succeeded by his son Chatri (or Tang Yue Hang), the present taipan. Bangkok Bank is considered to be one of the best managed in the country, and is certainly the largest in terms of assets. Profit growth averages around 50% per annum, and even if Thailand opens its banking system to foreign competition, the bank will maintain its edge.

At the moment, Chatri is working hard to pass the business on to his children without stirring up family squabbles. The eldest member of this third generation, Chatsiri, is clearly the son nominated as heir apparent, and currently cutting his teeth as executive vice-president of Bangkok Bank. Chali, the second son, is in charge of property assets and development, through the unlisted operation, City Realty, and is also responsible for the stockbroking operation, Asia Securities Trading. Union Asia Finance is run by Chatri's daughter, Sawitree, who is considered to be doing an exemplary job. The foundations for further serious diversification and expansion can be found in the other interests the family owns through Bangkok Bank, including chunks of shareholdings in Bangkok Insurance, Asia Credit, Bangkok First Investment & Trust, Thai Financial Syndicate, Krungdhep Warehouse, United Palm Oil Industry, the Bamrungrad Hospital, Charoong Thai Wire and Cable, Union Plastic, the NTS Steel Group and Bangkok Steel Industry.

Bangkok Land's Kanjanapas family, headed by taipan Mongkol (or Wong Chue Meng), has a net worth of approximately $1.6 billion, and amongst other assets owns a satellite city outside Bangkok. The family's unlisted finance arm is based in the Muang Thong Trust. The empire began three decades ago with a watch repair shop in Chinatown, from which Mongkol diversified into broadcasting, publishing, finance, hotels (Rajdamri Hotel) and property. Also under their umbrella is the Hong Kong-listed company, Stelux Holdings. They have had family-related business troubles, however, with Sakorn Kanjanapas resigning from the corporation when he was mentioned in an investigation that alleged mishandling of Siam City Bank stock. The company sold its stock in the bank in 1983, but is believed to be trying to get back into banking. The Kanjanapas brood is thought to be closer than most to the Thai military.

Despite these problems, those who know the family well say that the company is in very good hands, even with the sibling rivalry between Mongkol's sons, Anand, running Bangkok Land, and Keeree, running Tanayong, also a property company. Both men enjoy the limelight and relish the attention that their commercial activities bring them. At least, thanks to Mongkol's foresight, they have their own territories on which to leave their mark. Such is the extent of their competition, however, that they are both battling it out to build separate mass transit systems in their home city. They are also currently engaged in developing a huge residential complex in Beijing.

The Ratanaraks, another Sino-Thai family, are worth more than $1 billion and have a 26% stake in the family-run Bank of Ayudhya, which was founded in 1945 and is currently expanding into China, Vietnam and North America. They are also significantly involved in cement (Siam City Cement), life and other insurance, financial services, wheat flour production, television broadcasting, and the manufacture of bathroom fixtures, concrete, tiles and piping. The group's founder, Chuan Ratanarak, was succeeded in 1993 by his son, Krit, whose low-profile and secretive management style is much like his father's.

Finally, Banthoon Lamsam, whose family originally came from Guangdong province, controls the country's second largest bank, the Thai Farmers' Bank, which was founded by his father. Originally, the family started out in the logging business, but then diversified into insurance, rice and general trading. Banthoon is planning to expand into travel, the development of industrial estates, and department stores in mainland China.

(iv) SINGAPORE AND MALAYSIA

To many Western businessmen, Singapore and Malaysia might appear to be two of the least likely countries to provide a solid foundation for successful business. Lee Kuan Yew's re-invention of Singapore as a totalitarian dream, and Dr Mahathir's Islamic Malaysia do not good business make. Not so. There are in these two countries more than three dozen outstanding taipans, who are beginning to take a more influential position on the world economic stage.

The opportunities for doing business in both countries are legion. Malaysia, for example, has an abundance of natural resources, such as petroleum, tin, rubber and palm oil, and plentiful land to devote to agriculture. Her roads and ports are already well established. Shipments of oil and gas account for around 11% of export revenues, and petroleum has helped Malaysia diversify its export base away from agricultural commodities: although it is the producer of 60% of the world's palm oil and 25% of its rubber, commodities, together with oil and gas, now make up just one-third of exports. Manufacturing is the jewel in Malaysia's crown, growing at 11.5% a year and imminently expected to reach 33% of GDP. The export of manufactured goods, about half of them from the electronics sector, is increasing by 16.7% a year and should account for 75% of exports when the current five-year spending plan has run its course.

By comparison, what Singapore lacks in its own territory, it can cheaply and efficiently bring in from just next door. The country is fast becoming the pre-eminent centre in the Pacific Rim for high technology and communications. Both countries, though, are short on manpower. Fifteen years ago, Malaysia formulated a scheme to increase the population by the end of this century to the seventy million level, a feat which in reality it has very little chance of achieving. At the same time, Singapore masterminded a plan to keep the numbers down, a policy which has now had to be reversed.

For a long time, the two countries, in their desire to shake off their colonial pasts, were bound together in an economic interdependence. Malaysia, which constitutes the bottom half of the Malay peninsula, was known in colonial times and in the first few years of independence as Malaya. When the top quarter of the island of Borneo was incorporated into the country in 1963, the name was changed. Lee Kuan Yew's Singapore joined the Malaysian federation the same year, but split off as a tiny independent state two years later.

The entrepreneurial backbone of each country has been formed by just one man: in Singapore's case, by former prime minister Lee Kuan Yew; in Malaysia, by Datuk Seri Mahathir Mohamad, now in his thirteenth year as prime minister. Dr Mahathir comes from the permanent ruling party, the United Malays National Organization (UMNO). Both men are highly intelligent autocrats who have ruthlessly quashed even the slightest sign of dissent in order to achieve their ultimate end: national development. Their personal character foibles aside, both are due a great deal of admiration as patrons of their countries' burgeoning businesses.

While Singapore has the economic edge in having arrived at the heady status of an NIC (newly industrialised country) quite some time ago, Malaysia is set to pip current favourite Thailand to become Asia's next NIC. This is dependent, analysts say, upon whether Mahathir can get the country to follow through on development blueprints contained in a $37 billion five-year spending plan. The Fifth and Sixth Malaysia Plans have been designed to 'create a policy and implement programmes to sustain socioeconomic development and to ensure long-term economic stability'. An energetic leader, Mahathir has a vision of Malaysia becoming a fully developed country by the year 2020. By Third World standards, it is already rich: half of all households in Kuala Lumpur, for example, own a car. According to World Bank figures the percentage of Malaysians living below the official poverty line has already fallen impressively – from 37% in 1973 to around 15% today – and is still falling. Industry and entrepreneurship are seen as the main engines of growth.

Like many other businessmen in ex-colonial countries, the taipans of Malaysia and Singapore were quick to realise that their economies were growing much faster than those of their erstwhile masters. The taipans generally perceive the worldwide recession and the constant tales of unrest and strikes as being a major sign of the West's backward slide. This is not something they view with particular glee – they are after all losing lucrative markets – but simply as a matter of fact. When they look around their own region, they are well aware of the continued economic growth trend that surrounds them. It could be, they argue, that they are witness to nothing less than the shift of power to the Asian-Pacific Rim, a phenomenon from which their businesses can only benefit. It is very hard to disagree.

If the taipans want further evidence of this trend, they need only remind themselves that Asia, excluding Japan, has drawn up plans to spend in excess of $1 trillion on infrastructural projects alone in the next ten years. Perhaps that is why, they conclude, there is suddenly so much apparent kow-towing in their direction these days. No longer are Asians banging on doors in the US, Australia and Europe to sell their goods. This is substantiated in many ways, not the least of which is that US investment in Malaysia has been growing steadily since the early 1970s. Unlike the Japanese-owned factories in the country, which are supervised by cadres of managers and experts from Japan, many of the American-owned plants are run top to bottom by Malaysian citizens, many of whom will become the next generation of taipans.

Total US investment in Malaysia now ranks fourth after Singapore, Japan and the United Kingdom. Foreign companies and investment contribute significantly to the country's industrial development, taking the lead in a number of sectors, including petroleum and coal, chemical products, paper, printing and publishing, electrical and electronic products, and beverages and tobacco. Malaysia nevertheless likes its foreign business community to be transient and so insists that Malays hold at least a 30% stake in listed companies. In 1970, foreigners owned roughly 60% of the shares in local companies; Chinese held 30%; Malays less than 2%. The proportion of Malay-owned stock has since increased tenfold.

It is widely expected that by the end of the 1990s, foreign investment in Malaysia will be evenly distributed between Kuala Lumpur, Penang and Johore. Johore, on the southern tip of the peninsula and across the causeway from Singapore, has attracted numerous companies escaping from Singapore's high wages and appreciating currency. Currently, Kuala Lumpur leads, but Penang, Malaysia's silicon valley, is close behind. A mainly Chinese island, Penang is popular with the Chinese-speaking people of Taiwan, who are serious investors in the country. Scores of high-tech multinational companies, such as Hitachi, Intel, Motorola, Philips, Thomson, Sony and Advanced Micro Devices, have set up in Penang's industrial parks. The island, more than anywhere else, embodies Malaysia's harmonious blend of old and new, tropical and temperate. Even Georgetown, its business hub, has changed little since the first East

India Company settlement was founded there over two hundred years ago.

Penang's chief minister, Koh Tsu Koon, has gone to great lengths to establish the island as a regional centre for services and technology, encouraging international companies to take advantage of the skilled labour available there. Koh's success, which relies heavily on the educated Chinese population, has been such that he is now redirecting investors with labour-intensive industries towards other areas, such as Thailand and Indonesia. Penang is said to be about 20% richer than Malaysia as a whole.

Prime Minister Mahathir's long-running spat with Britain came to an end in 1988 with a $1.6 billion contract for British defence equipment. Mahathir had insisted in his Buy British Last policy that his country look to Japan for inspiration and investment. This was no doubt largely due to the fact that in 1981 relations with Britain had reached an all-time low when tuition fees were raised for all foreign students studying in Britain – of whom the 15,000 Malaysians constituted the single largest national contingent.

There was a feeling in Malaysia that people must stop being 'brown sahibs' and instead find their Asian roots. Malaysia is still hypersensitive about all comments made about it by other governments, but at least there is now a conviction that being Malay is a worthwhile pursuit.

Heir apparent to Mahathir is Anwar Ibrahim, a former radical Islamic activist and student leader who is now considered to be in the camp of big business. UMNO controls Malaysian politics to such an extent that the deputy president of the party is automatically the country's deputy prime minister and will succeed the outgoing president, who is also the prime minister. Anwar is taking a slightly harder line than Mahathir, arguing that he does not believe in allowing people to pass exams they have actually failed just because they are Malay. In his mind, the same applies in business. If a company does not fulfil a contract, he will give it to those who can, regardless of race. Good business sense is gaining the upper hand. Anwar is strident in his views, recently stating: 'We believe the foreign media must learn that developing countries, including a country led by a brown Muslim, have the ability to manage their own affairs successfully.'

Politics and business usually go hand in hand in Malaysia, with the politicians unafraid to flex their business muscles. As yet, the taipans have not flexed their political muscles. The companies that tend to perform best in the stock market are often those allied to political personalities whose fortunes are rising. Sometimes it is a matter of the politicians themselves boosting the stocks to raise funds for their campaigning. Other times the word spreads that a key figure is involved with a company, and the gossip machine does the rest. One well-known company was recently used in this way in a major takeover bid, and was then seen to benefit from a number of government-awarded contracts. While definitely not ethical, the practice is widespread. It is argued that if such things are going to happen anyway, a canny businessman might as well cash in.

The industrial development of two nations which were once politically united has differed in many ways, and so therefore has the growth of the taipans' commercial domains. Following its independence from Malaysia, Singapore fostered policies that favoured free enterprise and emphasised small businesses and entrepreneurship. The Singapore Economic Development Board, for example, makes sure that new businesses are helped in every way possible. Singapore is a melting pot of people from different social, racial, linguistic and religious backgrounds. Among the entrepreneurs, the Chinese and the Indians dominate.

For the last ten years the Malaysian government has also had a programme to stimulate private sector investment, which allows manufacturing firms with fewer than fifty employees to operate without a licence. They are also given very favourable tax incentives to comply. The conditions are those that taipans dream of, so much so that Hong Kong business people who know the region well often talk of moving to Kuala Lumpur in 1997.

It is generally agreed, though, that Singapore is the cleanest, safest, and most comfortable metropolis in Asia. Lee Kuan Yew's paternalistic and authoritarian methods, which are being continued by his successor, Goh Chok Tong, have made the country clean and efficient, with a conscious moral code that binds the people together. Many outsiders argue that the place is sterile, especially given its multicultural influences, very few traces of which are now obvious. They also claim that there is no freedom. It is true you are not free to urinate in the street or to drop litter, but you are at liberty to go about your business of making millions with as much help as the bureaucracy can give you – which is nearly always a great deal. What is good for business is good for the future of Singapore.

Like all the taipans, those from Singapore are a discreet bunch, averse to publicity of any sort and preferring to carry out their corporate plans without others prying into their affairs, especially when there are areas that might, in their opinion, be better glossed over. Kwek Hong Png, for example, was found guilty a couple of years ago of helping his nephew commit criminal breach of trust, and was heavily fined. Kwek and his son, Kwek Leng Beng, who founded the Hong Leong group, are the most significant of Singapore's taipans. The Singapore Kweks are related to the Queks of Malaysia, who have interests there in manufacturing, property and finance. The low-profile, cigar-smoking taipan, Quek Leng Chan, is a former lawyer, who together with his family owns 57.2% of Hong Leong (Malaysia) and is involved in manufacturing, construction and the financial sector, including the recently acquired financial arm of MUI (Malayan United Industries). The family also controls Hong Kong's Guoco group, which includes the Dao Heng Bank. Quek was involved in a record-setting buyout of the publishing group, New Straits Times, and of Sistem Telvisyen Malaysia through its Malaysian Resources Corporation. The two branches of the family own shares in each other's companies, but do not get on especially well in spite of their blood connection. The Kweks are said to be worth around $1 billion, while the Queks can 'only' notch up around $700 million. Competition between the two sides is fierce.

Kwek Hong Png's Hong Leong group of property and banking interests started commercial empire-building in 1963. In the 1960s and 1970s the group was an intricate web of cross-holdings designed to stop errant members of the family from cashing in on their shares. The Kweks moved stealthily through the property market and then on into financial services. Today, City Developments, which they control with a 50% share, is one of the largest land bank owners in Singapore. Also in the portfolio are a number of hotels in China, including the Holiday Inn in Xiamen. They own Hong Leong Finance, one of the largest single finance companies listed on the Singapore stock exchange. The group also has a hotel arm, CDL Hotels and CDL Hotels New Zealand, and they own the CDL Hotels (Chelsea) group and 37.5% of the Nikko Hotel in Hong Kong.

The $1-billion-plus fortune of Singapore's venerable Lee family consists of a major interest in the Oversea-Chinese Banking

Corporation, plus vast, long-held rubber plantations in the neigh-bouring Malaysian state of Johore. Lee Seng Wee, the taipan, is the son of Lee Kong Chian, who started out in the rubber, oil palm and pineapple businesses before moving into the finance sector. The bank, which was started before the war, is used by much of the Chinese population of Singapore. It is now run by a former cabinet minister, Dr Tony Tan, who is concentrating on developing its land assets to capitalise on its value. OCBC also owns OCBC Securities, and has interests in the food and drink group Fraser & Neave, Asian Pacific Breweries, Coca Cola Indochina, Bottlers Nepal, Robinsons the department store, Singapore Press Holdings and Times Pub-lishing.

Another key Singaporean family, very similar in history to the Lees, are the Wees. They are also heavily involved in banking, with the United Overseas Bank group, started by Wee Cho Yaw, which today includes 26% of Kay Hian James Capel stockbrokers; interests in securities companies in Hong Kong and elsewhere; ownership of the Chung Kiaw Bank, the Lee Wah Bank and the United Merchant Bank; and part ownership of the Industrial Commercial Bank and the Far Eastern Bank. Apart from its legion banking interests, the group owns the UOB Building, UOB Plaza and Alexandra Plaza in Singapore.

Many Malaysians today are descended from people who came to the country from elsewhere during the past hundred years, including India, Sumatra, Java and, of course, mainland China. This has resulted in a number of third- and fourth-generation citizens who, while not ethnically Malay, feel justified in having a deep and con-tinued involvement in the country and in their right to provide themselves and their families with a decent living. The 10% of the population that is made up of Indian Malaysians finds itself caught between the Malays and the Chinese. Their answer is to keep their heads down and concentrate on business. The Chinese, in contrast, make up 35 to 40% of the total population. This is enough to make them unignorable, but in the polarised racial politics of Malaysia, it has not been enough to persuade the Malays, who make up about half the population, to give them even a tiny share of political power.

There have always been fears about the Chinese, in both Singapore and Malaysia — that is, fears apart from those born out of material envy. These can only have been exacerbated in Malaysia by the fact that until very recently there were still one thousand or so Chinese guerrillas, members of the Malay Communist Party, in the jungles along Malaysia's northern border with Thailand. They financed their activities from logging in Thailand and from protection money extorted from Chinese-owned businesses in northern Malaysia. Not long ago, however, their leader, the legendary Chin Peng, decided from his operational HQ in mainland China that after forty-one years he would abandon the struggle and sign a peace agreement in Bangkok. He was no longer equal to the fight against the material success that his opponents had achieved.

Malaysia's prime minister, Dr Mahathir bin Mohamad, first came to the attention of the rest of the world in the late 1960s, when he wrote a highly controversial book entitled *The Malay Dilemma*. At the time, the country had just seen major race riots take place in which hundreds of people, mostly Chinese, were brutally murdered. The Chinese have naturally found themselves to be dominant in the country's economy, and palpable signs of their hard work were everywhere, causing massive resentment. How could so few, the locals demanded, have so much when they themselves had nothing? Mahathir replied that the Chinese were thriving because they had so many natural advantages. In his opinion, 'Whatever the Malays could do, the Chinese could do better.' Fair competition, he maintained, was therefore not possible, and to counter this imbalance, he would have to implement a policy that would favour the 'bumiputera' ('sons of the soil').

The result was a New Economic Policy, which introduced a mammoth programme of positive discrimination, with quotas that were severely biased in favour of the Malays and very much against the Chinese and Indian sections of the population. Up until very recently non-bumiputeras have been required to pay more for mortgages and other government-assisted services than native Malays. Of the tens of thousands of students from Malaysia who study abroad, most are bumiputeras, such is the bias in granting scholarships. The upshot is that the Indians and Chinese have had to sweat that much harder and longer for every educational or economic achievement they have accomplished.

As émigrés, or sons or grandsons of émigrés, the taipans have all been handed down stories of how hard life was in China or India, an existence of continual poverty, famine and flood. In their adopted homeland, however, though life might be tough, they at least had some opportunity to learn, work, raise a family and develop a business that could be handed down to future generations. However small that opportunity might be, it had to be capitalised on. That was the ideal that has kept them going and made them not only survivors but success stories.

Ironically one of the main motivations in Malaysia for Chinese and Indian success has been the creation of the class of Malay 'fat cats'. The Chinese argue that the Malays are ridiculously advantaged, not only in business but also when it comes to private life. Malay children are positively eased into university, even when they obviously fail to make the required grade. In corporate life, Malay companies do not have to declare ownership by nominees and there is far greater flexibility with quotas and in other areas of compliance if it can be shown that the management of a company is bumiputera-dominated. The net result is that while the Malays are still, on average, poorer than the Chinese, there is now a new Malay middle class in business and society, the creation of which has helped considerably to weaken the old resentments and humiliations.

In the late 1980s, triggered by Chinese unrest arising from fears that a change in the school system might mean the end of Mandarin-language education, Mahathir instituted another political crackdown. This entailed a press law, giving him arbitrary and unlimited powers to ban journalists or articles that he did not like. Lee Kuan Yew made similar attacks on the Fourth Estate as and when he saw fit, throwing out non-compliant journalists from the *Far Eastern Economic Review* on a mere whim. The control of the press in Malaysia and Singapore meant that all opposition was suppressed and the people were marshalled back into order. Corruption, especially in Malaysia, was common, but businessmen went about their business regardless.

The fifteen largest corporate structures in Malaysia account for 68% of the stockmarket's capitalisation, and it is from these companies, and a few others, that the country's taipans come. The main conglomerates are Renong, Multi-Purpose, Sime Darby and the Hong Leong group. The gaming sector includes Genting Berhad, Tanjong, Berjaya Sports Toto, and Permodalan Nasional Berhad, which holds key interests in finance, plantation, and property companies on behalf of the National Bumiputera Unit Trust Scheme.

One business deal that highlights the *modus operandi* of the country and its taipans is a vast $1.2 billion scheme expected to last twenty years. Touted as the single largest new property development in the world today, the architect is the American, Cesar Pelli, who designed

174

Canary Wharf in London's Docklands. The ambitious scheme, the Kuala Lumpur City Centre Project, is the brainchild of taipan Ananda Krishnan, and is vocally backed by Dr Mahathir. Until about eight years ago, Ananda Krishnan was deeply involved in Malaysia's national oil company, Petronas. Today he operates through the former tin-mining company, Tanjong, which was relisted on both the Kuala Lumpur and London stock exchanges in 1991 and now holds the licence for Malaysia's national tote. Another Krishnan company, Binariang, has interests in telecommunications, including mobile and international phone licences.

The project revolves around the redevelopment of a one-hundred-acre town-centre site in Kuala Lumpur on the site of the old racecourse. The first phase of the scheme, which will add 6.1 million square feet of office space by 1996, includes a luxury hotel, a huge shopping centre with a multistorey Japanese Sogo department store, apartments, and four office blocks (including two eighty-five-storey towers). The required infrastructure of roads, underpasses and a light railway will completely alter the centre of the city. The main tenant in the tower blocks is Petronas, which also owns 50% of the site development company. If there are insufficient tenants – the main reason for Canary Wharf's problems – Krishnan can simply call on his good friend the prime minister and get the government to move in.

Vincent Tan Chee Yioun, a dapper businessman who is not afraid of visibility in the markets, owns 13% of the Berjaya group and is, apart from Robert Kuok, Malaysia's most high-profile new taipan. Twenty years ago, he acquired the McDonald's franchise for the country, and he has also enjoyed great success with the Singer franchise. Berjaya Sports Toto, which he bought ten years ago, when the Malaysian government embarked on its privatisation scheme, is now a healthy division of Berjaya Leisure. The group also owns 60% of the very lucrative Berjaya Lottery Management (HK) Ltd, which runs the national lottery. Also on the gaming front, the unassuming taipan Lim Goh Tong, who was born in Anwei, Fujian, and who made his billions originally in iron mining and construction, now owns 51% of the conglomerate Genting International Ltd – owners of the Burswood casino in Australia – and 40% of Genting Bhd, with its subsidiaries Resorts World and Asiatic Development, which owns theme parks and plantations.

One of the best-known Malaysian taipans active in Hong Kong

is Teh Hong Piow, a prominent businessman who controls Public Bank, Malaysia's leading commercial bank. He used to be chairman in Hong Kong of First Shanghai Investments, until he was succeeded by Madam Chen Weili, the daughter of the veteran Chinese Communist leader, Chen Yun.

The family of the late Lee Loy Seng own 42.2% of the Kuala Kepong group, and the three sons now own and run the largest oil palm, rubber and cocoa plantation operations in the country, after those of Sime Darby and PNB. The four listed companies of the Lee group are Glenealy Plantations (Malaya) Bhd, Batu Kawan Berhad, Kuala Lumpur Kepong (KLK) and Parit Perak. Tan Sri Dato' (Dr) Loy Hean Heong owns 32.6% of MBF Holdings and is president and CEO of the group, which has offices in Hong Kong, China, Taiwan, Thailand, Vietnam and the United States. The group itself has interests in everything from finance to education and property management.

William Cheng owns 10.6% of ASM, now the largest steel mill in Malaysia, through his 41.2% stake in the Lion group, as well as six other listed companies, including Klang Securities, Parkson Stores, Subang Parade and Sabah Gas Industries. The turnaround of Sabah Shipyard, formerly a government-owned entity, brought Joseph Chong and his holding company Westmont Holdings into prominence only a couple of years ago. He has now branched out overseas into the Philippines and China, where he is pursuing interests in steel, banking, power generation and horse-racing.

As discussed earlier, the bumiputeras have done very well in Malaysia in recent years. An outstanding example is Tan Sri Dato' Abdul Rashid bin Hussain, the country's best-known stockbroker. Now the largest broker in the country, Rashid Hussain was involved in setting up the Kuala Lumpur Options and Futures Exchange. His company also owns 20% of D&C Bank, through which Hussain has diversified into other activities, such as financial management and consultancy, property, and computer software. Another bumiputera taipan is Samsudin Abu Hassan, who, in concert with Teh Soon Seng, was behind the listing of the timber company Aokam Perdana in 1992. He now also has interests in Granite Industries, Cold Storage and Landmark.

Tunku Tan Sri Dato' Seri Ahmad Yahaya, who is connected politically at the highest levels, has a 74.8% interest in the DRB group (Diversified Resources Bhd), the makers with Proton of a popular two-door sports car. His corporate vehicle is Master Carriage and he also has a stake in Gadek (Malaysia) Bhd. The latter company has acquired a 90% share in the huge finance company, Credit Corporation Malaysia Bhd, and is looking to expand into the insurance business. Yahaya Ahmad ran Sime Darby for a long time, but has retired in favour of his deputy chairman, Encik Nik Mohamed Yaacob, who is continuing to run Malaysia's oldest and most professional conglomerate along traditional lines. Sime Darby is a major bumiputera company, owned through the country's largest trust fund, which was set up to promote Malay economic and commercial interests.

Wan Azmi Bin Wan Hamzah is considered to be one of the most talented managers in Malaysia, and is among the most respected and well connected of bumiputera taipans. He controls 20.7% of diversified Land & General Bhd, a significant property player, and 13.1% of cigarette manufacturer R. J. Reynolds Bhd. He exercises managerial supervision and control over both groups of companies. Through Land & General, Wan Azmi also has interests in the manufacture of PVC, banking, securities and the timber industry, and a 19.99% interest in the Australian-listed company Odin Mining and Investment. He also owns 25% of Rashid Hussain, the securities firm.

Former Malaysian finance minister, Daim Zainuddin, has had a number of very successful protégés, including Tajuddin Ramli of the TRI group (Technology Resources Industries Bhd), who was once the CEO of Utama Wardley merchant bank. Ramli bought an interest in Raleigh with some friends, and went on to acquire a 51% stake in Celcom from Telekom Malaysia. Today he controls 32% of Malaysian Airline System Bhd, the national airline, through his 13% ownership of Malaysian Helicopter Services Bhd. Another protégé is Halim Saad, who now controls 37.8% of the Renong Group, which owns nine listed companies. Included in the stable of interests are the contractors United Engineers (UEM), the North-South Expressway privatisation project, TIME, Southern Steel, Kinta Kellas, Ho Hup, and CIMA, the cement manufacturer. Halim Saad also has a 60% stake in the urban toll road operator, Metacorp.

Tan Sri Dato Asman Hashim owns 60% of the Arab-Malaysian Corporation and is a former director of Malayan Banking Bhd, the country's largest commercial bank. An accountant by training, Asman went on to become chairman of the Kwong Yik Bank and then joined AMMB, which is now Malaysia's largest and most profitable bank. AM Corp. has a number of subsidiaries, including a holding company, a merchant bank, a finance company, a credit bank, a securities holding company, life insurance interests, a development company and a property trust. It also has one overseas company, Security Pacific Asian Bank, which has just one branch.

Mohamed Ghazali Mohamed Khalid is involved with seven listed companies and is one of the most popular of bumiputera partners for the Chinese taipans when they are going for a listing on the Malaysian stock exchange. He is on the boards of Denko, Mah Sing, Golden Frontier, Super Enterprise, and U-Wood, and is executive chairman of the Pahang-based Mentiga Corporation group, a timber company and the largest maker of prefabricated houses in the country.

The two royal princes of the Negri Sembilan royal family, Tunku Naquiyuddin and Tunku Imran, are the powers behind Antah Holdings Bhd, in which they have a 20% stake. With activities in manufacturing and the financial and food sectors, the company began life fifteen years ago as Syarikat Pesaka Antah Sdn Bhd. Its fortunes were greatly advanced by Dr Mahathir's bumiputera programme. Antah owns 32% of a UK-listed company, Unigroup PLC, which in turn owns nearly 95% of Golden Pharos Bhd.

The Malay royal family hover on the periphery of business in that country. While they are by no means taipans, they have been instrumental in many cases in creating taipans out of others. Malaysia's Chinese businessmen, for example, have often operated as hidden partners to the profiteering royals.

Each of Malaysia's thirteen states has a constitutional monarch, whose status was unaffected by independence in 1957. Even though the country was to be run by a government and a prime minister, there was little change to the sultans' powers. Immune to all national law, the sultans lorded it over their territories, abusing their power without compunction. Eventually, Mahathir, who had never liked the idea of the monarchs, decided to act to curb their powers. For the first time, legislation was enacted to stop the sultans' immunity from prosecution, and it was made clear that civil servants, who in the past had pandered to their whims, were no longer to indulge them. Free from the constraints of royal favouritism, Malaysia's new taipans are now free to rule their commercial domains on merit alone.

Li, Ka Shing & Family of Hong Kong

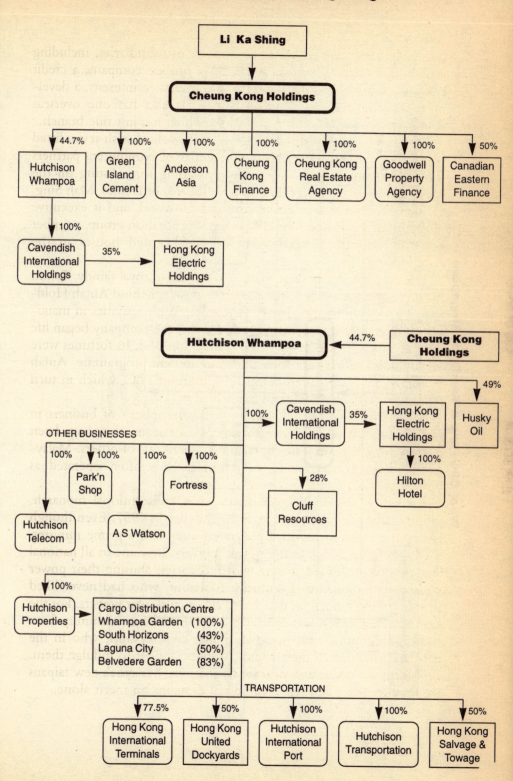

Wee, Cho Haw & Family of Singapore

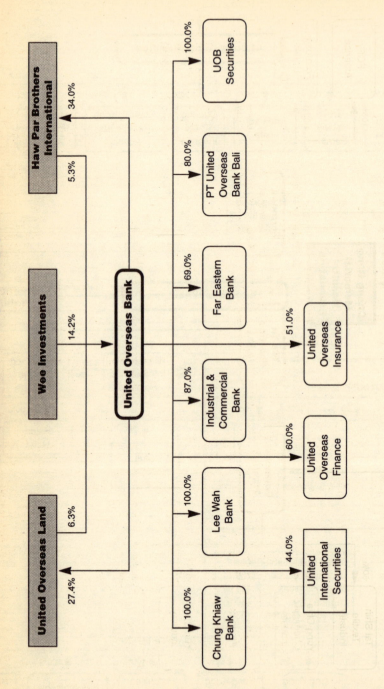

Wang, Yungching & Family of Taiwan

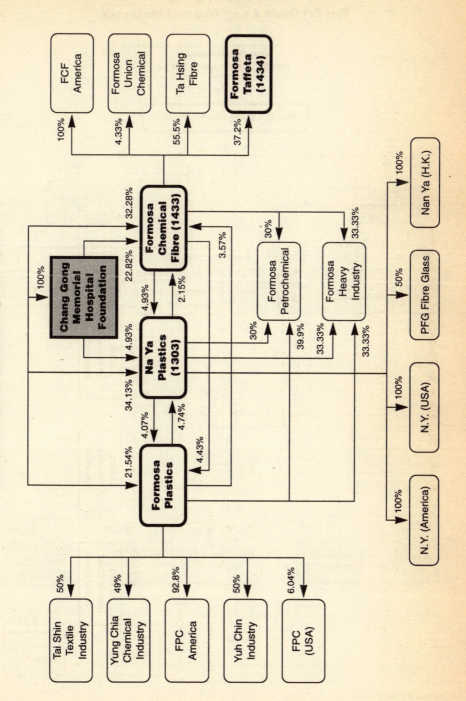

The Quek Family
Tan Sri Quek Leng Chan of Malaysia

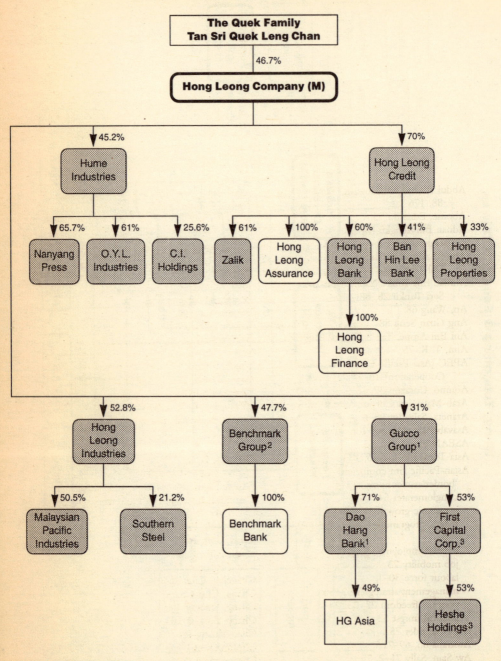

1 Listed in Hong Kong
2 Listed in the UK
3 Listed in Singapore

Index

183